Pre-Grouping Trains on
BRITISH RAILWAYS

The LMS Companies

Frontispiece: Derby, 1952. This 1924 Compound sums up the early BR years and is also typical of early LMS days. It was built in 1924 and although there have been detail changes it still looks Midland in style. Its new owners have renumbered it and that is the only evidence of nationalisation anywhere in this scene.

Pre-Grouping Trains on
BRITISH RAILWAYS

The LMS Companies

Peter Hay

Oxford Publishing Co.

A FOULIS-OPC Railway Book

Typesetting by:
Colin Powell Typesetting & Design, Bournemouth, Dorset.

Published by:
Haynes Publishing Group
Sparkford, Near Yeovil, Somerset. BA22 7JJ

Haynes Publications Inc.
861 Lawrence Drive, Newbury Park, California 91320, USA

British Library Cataloguing in Publication Data
Pre-grouping trains on British Railways :
  the LMS companies.
  1. London, Midland and Scottish Railway
  2. Locomotives—Great Britain—
  History
  I. Hay, Peter, *1932-*
  625.2'61'0941   TJ603.4.G72L65
  ISBN 0-86093-394-6

Contents

Bibliography

Midland Style	Historical Model Railway Society
The Midland Railway	C.Hamilton Ellis
The Somerset & Dorset Railway	R.Atthill
The Midland Compounds	D.F.Tee / R.C.T.S.
London Tilbury & Southend Locomotives	C.Langley Aldrich
Great Central *(for C.L.C.)*	George Dow
Premier Line	O.S.Nock
The Furness Railway	R.W.Rush
The North Staffordshire Railway	'Manifold'
The Lancashire & Yorkshire Railway *(3 vols)*	John Marshall
The Lancashire & Yorkshire Railway in the Twentieth Century	Eric Mason
Railways Around East Lancashire	C.R.Wilby
The Caledonian Railway	O.S.Nock
Caledonian Railway Centenary	Stephenson Locomotive Society
The Caledonian Dunalastairs	O.S.Nock
40 Years of Caledonian Locomotives	H.J.Campbell Cornwell
Tales of the Glasgow & South Western Railway	David L.Smith
Legends of the Glasgow & South Western Railway in LMS Days	David L. Smith
The Glasgow & South Western Railway	Stephenson Locomotive Society
The Highland Railway	H.A.Vallance
The Highland Railway, Constituents and Successors	Stephenson Locomotive Society
Illustrated History of LMS Locomotives	} R.J.Essery and D.Jenkinson
Illustrated History of LMS Coaches	
A Pictorial Record of LMS Signals	Warburton and Anderson
Railway Steam Cranes	J.S.Brownlie
Clinker's Register of Closed Stations	C.R.Clinker
Bradshaw	
The Railway Observer	Railway Correspondence & Travel Society
The Journal of the Stephenson Locomotive Society	
Railway Junction Diagrams	Railway Clearing House

Plate 1: The Caledonian Railway '812' class 0-6-0s became something of a standard product on the LMS lines in Scotland, taking over from scrapped GSWR and Highland engines. No. 57613 is on its home ground as it moves a heavy train loaded with iron and steel, products of local industry, across Lesmahagow Junction, at Motherwell, in April 1960, sixty years after its building by Dubs & Co. of Glasgow. This class was J.F.McIntosh's advance on the Drummond 'Jumbos' of the 1880s, but both classes survived together almost until the end of steam in Scotland.

Preface

In the amount of surviving railway equipment of pre-grouping design, the areas once served by the LMS occupied a position midway between the famine situation on the former GWR — where what little that did survive had been comprehensively remoulded into the Great Western image — and the LNER and SR areas where there were feasts awaiting the lovers of pre-grouping relics. This book is not a comprehensive survey, but rather the results of my own and other people's awareness that such things would be gone forever, one day not far distant, and that we had better get a photographic record of them while they were still around. In 1923, the LMS had taken over railways that were just as varied in their diversity as those that formed the LNER group but, by 1948, had gone further than the LNER in providing them with modern equipment of its own designs. This may have been due to the quality of the LMS inheritance which was patchy, to call it no worse, as well as to the events of the 1920s in the Chief Mechanical Engineer's Department. The latter are well-known today, so I refer only briefly to them in the chapters on the various parts of the former LMS system. It is also true that the effectiveness of the LMS management increased over the years. As on the other 'Big Four' railways, World War II shortages gave extended life to what would otherwise have been replaced, and by the time British Railways took over on 1st January 1948, there was still quite a lot which was overdue for replacement. The pace of scrapping the old quickened as the economy slowly recovered from the war, but unhappily the shortages of 1948 to 1951 extended to film for our cameras. That is partly why I have sometimes been unsuccessful in finding working pictures of what was lost in those years. Without the unstinting kindness of many people, not all of whom provided pictures but who introduced me to those who could, this book would have many more regrettable omissions. The photographers and collectors whose pictures I have used are credited at the end of the caption (uncredited pictures are my own work, for better or worse) and here I record my sincere thanks to all who helped me so generously.

This book is divided into six chapters, each dealing with one of the major LMS constituents. Pre-1923 line ownership has been the criterion of what goes where, not the lineage of the rolling stock depicted. As explained in the text which introduces each chapter, scrapping by the LMS or BR sometimes caused equipment from one pre-grouping company to be used elsewhere. In addition to these transfers, there were the consequences of the LMS continuing in the 1920s to built to the old companies' designs, so some pre-grouping items have building dates after 1923. The Midland is a special case because of Derby's dominance in matters mechanical, so Midland-type rolling stock came to be found beyond the former MR boundaries, in the GSWR section particularly. In deciding where to include joint lines I have made my own rules. If only one of the partners came into the LMS, where to include the pictures is obvious. Where both pre-grouping partners joined the LMS I have been guided in general by the timetabled pattern of services.

Although these pictures are grouped in chapters, I have found it difficult to conceive a method of arranging them within the chapter which works in all six. Some readers may even find that the resulting randomness is enjoyable because they will not know what to expect on the next page. As to the captions, I have tried to make them informative without including too much of such detail as is easily available these days. Even so, the moment we turn away from the line or the locomotive, we become aware of how little has been published. Happily, the great growth of interest in modelling with passionate fidelity railways as they once were has made it possible for the real experts to publish their knowledge for the benefit of us all. It was not always so. In the 1950s there was almost nothing in detail published about carriages, wagons, signalling, or many other interesting remains, even though they could still be seen daily. Filling in those gaps in our knowledge continues, but our ignorance was once very great. When I took my pictures I sometimes recorded details of any old equipment on view, but it was recording by guesswork in many cases. For example I did not know what an LNWR carriage looked like, but learned to identify them from the axlebox covers. With today's detailed books at hand, how I wish I had recorded the carriage as well as the engine numbers, when I took a picture. This leads me to give a general caution about the captions. I have tried to be accurate, but I make no promises or claims to infallibility — rather the reverse. If you are sure my caption is wrong, you are almost certainly right although I hope you will allow that both our memories do have their lapses.

If I had written this book in the 1950s, I should not have been able to give the list of books which I have found specially useful for pre-grouping information, neither should I have needed to, because there were plenty of enthusiasts alive whose memories and records stretched back to the beginning of this century. My problem today is to remind myself that books I have grown up with may be long out of print and not easily obtained, but their value is acknowledged in many instances by publishers reprinting them, so you should be able to get a copy if your conviction that I have got the facts wrong drives you that hard.

I do not want to end, as seems the fashion today, by thanking everybody in sight including the cat, for their help, but there are two people besides the photographers who I will mention. They are Derek Mercer and Tim Shuttleworth, who have printed many of these pictures. Both deserve your thanks and mine for the way they have so often rescued my inept photography and made it fit to place before you.

Plate 2: The LMS briefly fitted front numberplates on the LNWR 0-8-0s, but BR never bothered. As the engines in their later years were cleaned only infrequently, identification could be a problem, but this member of the class is thought to be No. 49328, then shedded at Bescot (3A), waiting to leave Lichfield with a train for Walsall. In the spring of 1959, this class was still sufficiently common for the crew to find it noteworthy that someone should be taking a picture of them and their engine.

There are two reasons why the Midland Railway may appear to be over-represented in this book. The first is the multiplication of Midland locomotive designs by the LMS after 1923. This came about because the Motive Power Superintendent of the new company was J.E. Anderson, a former Midland man, as was Henry Fowler who took over in 1925 as Chief Mechanical Engineer. For many years the Midland's express passenger traffic had been dominated by the idea that the best way to compete — as the Midland always had to — was to provide a frequent service of trains. Because they were frequent none of them was heavy, and therefore generally within the ability of 4-4-0 type express engines. This system was the opposite of most other main lines, notably the east and west coast routes, where services were less frequent and trains much heavier in consequence. So the East Coast companies, and the LNW/Caledonian alliance, were gradually forced to build six-coupled types, much larger than the four-coupled engines on the Midland. The latter were, of course, enlarged as the years went by, and in the early years of this century under R.M. Deeley the standard Midland 4-4-0 was provided with a high-pitched Belpaire boiler giving a modern outline, but its power was in no way comparable to an LNWR 'George' or a Caledonian 'Dunalastair', neither did Midland enginemen habitually work their engines nearly so hard as was normal on the LNWR.

For its heaviest workings the MR mainly relied on a small band of 3-cylinder Compounds, the alternative being double-heading with two smaller 4-4-0s. When the LMS was formed in 1923, there followed trials of the Compounds against Caledonian four-coupled and LNWR six-coupled types. From these trials the Midland design emerged sufficiently superior (if not triumphant), for it to become the new standard. Now if the Midland's dominance of the LMS had been total there should have followed a wholesale rewriting of timetables all over the system, with 'light and frequent' being the new pattern of passenger services. It did not happen, so on the LNWR, at least, the Compounds which Derby was building were not used on the heavy long-distance trains but mainly kept to duties like the Birmingham services. Meanwhile, the 'Georges' and the 'Princes' thrashed along as usual with loads that would have a Midland driver weakly calling for assistance. The legions of new Compounds went to lines like the GSWR and the Caledonian (which latter had little need of them), and when in 1928 the LMS version of the standard Midland 4-4-0 simple appeared, they too were allocated far away from Derby. By that date there was indeed a need for a 'middleweight' 4-4-0, to replace some of the worn-out relics of Victorian times.

With goods engines, the story was a little different. The most modern MR 0-6-0 type, which dated from 1911, became the LMS standard six-coupled goods, a total of 580 being built down the years from 1924. But there were other LMS designs for goods work, a 2-6-0 (the 'Crab') in 1927, which were a product of Horwich thinking, and an 0-8-0 (the 'Austin 7'), which looked like a cross between a Midland 0-6-0 and an LNWR 0-8-0. However, despite these rival attractions, it would be true to say that Midland influence dominated new building in the first five years of the LMS, over 900 engines being produced. There were also over 400 0-6-0 shunting tanks based on a Midland 1899 design. When these numbers are added to the quantity of genuine MR engines, it is easy to realise why the 'Derby outline' survived so numerously into BR days. It was to be found the length and breadth of the LMS.

That length and breadth is the second reason why there is so much Midland-style equipment pictured in this book. The LMS proper was large, but it was made larger still by its participation in several joint lines, such as the Somerset & Dorset, which took LMS engines to Bournemouth as it had Midland types before them, and the Cheshire Lines Committee which took them to

Liverpool and Chester. I have thought it proper to include in this section pictures of workings on joint lines which were once partly Midland and later LMS. As the MR absorbed the London, Tilbury & Southend Railway in 1912, that too has been included, although for once the LMS perpetuated the local 'Tilbury' design until the 'Stanier revolution' of the 1930s.

For Londoners and southerners, of course, the Midland began at St. Pancras, and in the early BR years the comparison with the old Euston could not have been more stark. Whereas one was a complexity of platforms, barrriers, roads and offices, the other could not have been more simple. Once on to St. Pancras concourse, there was the station in its entirety, under one roof. Other London stations have all-over roofs, but none is so totally defining as Barlow's great arch. Even one's dimmest relations or most scatterbrained aunts could find the way. I suspect that nobody has ever got lost in St. Pancras Station, but it is rumoured that some of the more confused victims of the old Euston were only released from their wanderings when that station was demolished.

St. Pancras was the Midland Railway's grand gesture but, in my opinion, its true character was only to be experienced down in the shires. That is why there are no pictures of St. Pancras here, but several of Derby. Even great Crewe did not provide the same combination of heart and brain for the LNWR as Derby did for the Midland. As well as the advances in passengers' comfort and convenience masterminded by James Allport in the Victorian years, Derby was the birthplace of generations of excellent carriages under Clayton, David Bain, and R.W. Reid. Few other railways could match the system-wide quality of Midland coaching stock and, happily for the LMS, Reid was its first Carriage & Wagon Superintendent, so the carriages of the 1920s bore a close resemblance to the final Midland Railway designs, and many of them can be seen in these pictures.

Derby was also the birthplace of Midland locomotives, double-framed under Kirtley and elegant under S.W. Johnson. The mark of his successor, Richard Deeley, was the large cab with four front spectacle glasses which appeared, not only on his own designs, but on those of his predecessor as reboilering gave old engines a new lease of life. There are few Johnson engines in anything like original condition in these pictures, but many as rebuilt, reboilered, and recabbed by Deeley and Henry Fowler, who took over after Deeley stormed out in 1909. After George Hughes' brief spell as Chief Mechanical Engineer of the new LMS, Fowler got the job in 1925, and the Midland outline continued. All this, as well as the drive to London, the push to Carlisle, and such modern ideas as centralised traffic control, came from Derby. Sometimes there could be too much looking to Derby, for as late as the 1960s ex-Midland stations were being asked not to send the station bicycle to Derby Works for repair, but to take it to the shop down the High Street. Old habits died hard, and the Midland had no other centre than Derby.

Bedford is hardly in the Midlands, but travelling northwards from London (and of course, towards Derby) I felt that Bedford was where the real Midland flavour began, and the shape of a signal box roof or the design of a platform fence could signal its approach as London was left behind. It is therefore appropriate that I have included a glimpse back into the past in the form of the Bedford Telegraph Office (Plate 14). Although some of our 'Brighton' telephone switchboards were antiquated, I never saw anything like Bedford Telegraph Office on the Southern.

North from Bedford was the Northamptonshire ironstone district, and then began the realm of coal trains ('minerals', to give them their proper name), and a southerner was in a strange land. Any such area is likely to abound in short goods trips and local workings, giving useful employment to small freight engines, and in that way the army of small 0-6-0 tender engines which had been, in their time, the mainstay of the Midland's long-distance coal traffic, survived to a great age. Reboilering helped, and 70 years was not an unusual age for a MR 0-6-0 in early BR days. Some of them even retained the spring balance safety-valves.

Many of my journeys on the Midland main line took me to Manchester, through the shires to Derby and then over that delightful and exciting line now alas closed, through the heart of the Peak District. I always looked out for the Johnson 0-4-4 tank on the Buxton branch train at Miller's Dale, and shortly afterwards the train began its cautious circuit of Manchester to arrive in time at Central Station. Midland trains only reached there by virtue of the company's participation in the Cheshire Lines Committee, just as they reached Bournemouth by the Somerset & Dorset, or Yarmouth over the Midland & Great Northern Joint Railway. But only a concern so adept at railway diplomacy could have gone on to Lowestoft by a line that was jointly owned, not with another railway, but with another joint railway. Thus the Norfolk & Suffolk Joint Committee, where the M&GN Joint and the Great Eastern reined in their rivalry, shared the traffic from Lowestoft's fish quays, and courted the clientele of Cromer, select and withdrawn on the windy east coast.

Victorian writers about railways, when they came to discuss the Midland, often referred to the 'Midland Octopus', and a glance at the pre-grouping map shows why. From Swansea and Southport in the west, to Southend and Yarmouth in the east, from Bournemouth and Carlisle, Midland carriages and trains ran daily. By ownership, joint lines, and what the Railway Clearing House referred to as 'running powers and working arrangements', the Midland could get you almost anywhere. No wonder other railways, guarding their stretch of territory and concentrating their energies there, saw the Midland as an octopus. But we should

note that there was not a single place of any size where the Midland had the only station. Even in Derby it had to compete — admittedly only for local traffic — with the Great Northern. And so, octopus or not, the Midland was kept up to the mark by competition, until providing a uniformly good standard of service became a habit. Other railways surpassed it at their best, but away from the spotlight or the spur of competition, they fell far short. Only the North Eastern Railway, which had a virtual monopoly of its area, gave the same uniformly good service. The reasons for that were deep, and this is not the place to explore them, but if ever Midland men in secret and untrumpeted pride looked down on, for example, the lordly North Western, they surely regarded the North Eastern as a worthy equal.

In our time the various aspects of the MR have had somewhat patchy attention. The locomotive problems of the early grouping have been explored in detail, the excellence of carriages is now well-documented, and the more picturesque parts of the system, like the Settle & Carlisle line or the Somerset & Dorset, have been photographed extensively. The line through the High Peak, more spectacular if not so wild, attracted photographers less. The Cheshire Lines, where until nationalisation the engines were mostly ex-GCR, has had little attention compared to the Somerset & Dorset. My pictures in this chapter were taken, in some instances at least, almost as a by-product of interest in another pre-grouping company, as the Class 2P 4-4-0 leaving York *(Plate 12)* was taken while waiting for North Eastern engines. This haphazard approach has one virtue — it demonstrates how widely the old Midland Railway spread its influence, and how what happened in the early years of the LMS maintained and extended the area where Midland objects of all sorts were to be found. These pictures also show what a wealth of other MR equipment survived long after the LMS had become British Railways.

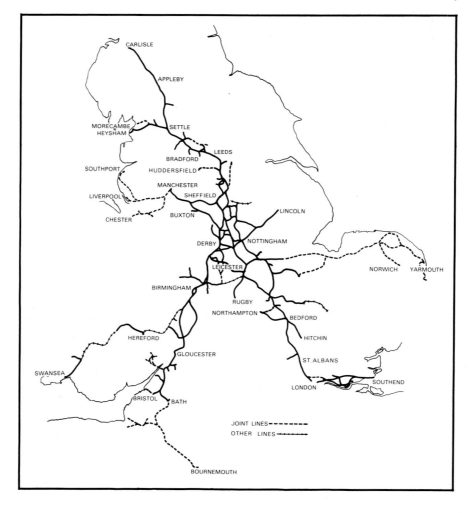

Plate 3: At the head of a Midland goods train there was invariably an 0-6-0 tender engine like No. 43321. As the platelayers stand back for a moment, it comes bustling along the through lines past Chesterfield Station, in 1957, with an early morning unfitted freight train. Deeley's arrangement of double spectacle glasses to go with the Belpaire firebox gave a much better lookout than the old pattern of a single round spectacle. On the left is a glimpse of something that seemed more common on the Midland than elsewhere — an old coach body grounded as an office, store, workshop, rest room or any other use that local railwaymen could think of.

Plate 4: A rectangular cab sidesheet panel supporting one with a cut-out was the common late Victorian cab style for tender engines (see *Plates 58 & 96* for the LNWR and L&Y varieties respectively). This old Johnson 0-6-0 had acquired a Belpaire boiler with pop valves but otherwise looked fairly original when it came to Derby for scrapping in 1952. Its previous boiler and safety-valve arrangements can be seen on the adjoining engine, also waiting for the torch.

Plate 5 (Above): The Deeley style of cab as applied to the small 0-6-0s of Johnson's design looks a little overpowering on this Class 2F as it trundles through Matlock in August 1953. This veteran of 1880 was given the new cab in 1920 and I am sure the enginemen appreciated it, especially if they did a lot of winter work in the Peak District. Matlock presented several other relics of the Midland Railway, among them being the sawn diagonal fencing and the standard of the gas lamp beside it.

Plate 7: A bit of 'old Midland' at Derby in 1952, in the robust form of three of Johnson's standard shunting tanks, each with the later Belpaire boiler. Three different liveries are in use — the first standard BR design is on No. 41795, the next engine is still LMS, and a blocklettered BRITISH RAILWAYS tank brings up the rear. Within the next couple of years variations like this pretty well disappeared, but in BR's early days there were some confusing varieties to be seen. This class was probably the last tank engine type in Britain to run with half instead of full cabs, and in rainy weather they were almost useless. The Midland Railway Trust at Butterley puts a winter back on to their No. (4)1708 these days. Notice the large iron tool box, too big for the cab, and exiled to the footplating, just waiting to trip somebody up on a dark night.

Plate 6 (Left): Early writers on railways were much impressed by 'the Trijunct station at Derby. It presents really an imposing sight. The light and lofty iron columns, the admirably contrived and elegant roofs, the spacious platforms — all unite in rendering it the most complete structure of the kind in the Kingdom, perhaps in the World'. Much enlarged by 1952, portions of this marvel still remained, especially on the left in this view. There are also some Midland lamp posts and a pillar water column, everything but the ghost of George Hudson who once lorded it over these platforms. He got a monumental snub from another railway potentate here too, just before his empire collapsed.

Plate 8 (Below): Inside Derby roundhouse the sun lights up a real antique, one of the early Johnson inside cylinder 0-4-0 tanks. Spring balance safety-valves were still fairly common at Derby in 1948, but how many engines had a cab so modest that the reversing lever stood outside in the open? This engine had been on the Departmental list since 1924.

F.W. Shuttleworth

Plate 9: Sand is pouring out of the pipe in front of the near driving wheel as an ancient MR 0-6-0 battles its way out of Williamsthorpe Colliery on the Grassmoor branch in Derbyshire. The angle between the line of the engine's footplating and that of the tender says something about the state of the track and the effort the engine is putting out, which has made it 'dig its tail in'. Before the days when all-steel coal wagons were universal, there were some pretty rugged-looking wooden specimens like those which are taking the strain in this 1955 picture.

BR/OPC Joint Venture

Plate 10: The LMS standard 0-6-0 shunting tank was derived from Midland originals of 1899, No. 47207 being one of the condensing variety for use on cross-London goods trains, via the 'widened lines'. It is on just such a duty, at Bricklayers Arms on the Southern, in March 1957, nearly sixty years later. This underground route ceased to be a freight artery long ago but is about to re-open for passenger services, which brings back memories of the Kentish Town to Victoria local trains of long ago, before there was ever a Victoria line, or any other line.

Plate 11: A Midland Compound far from home. No. 41167 was in fact one of the LMS-built 6ft. 9in. variety dating from 1925, and has the tall Stanier chimney. It went new to the Western Division (ex-LNWR) and from there it appeared north of Brighton with an excursion from Northampton in 1952. Although theoretically out of gauge, it was safely home again before anyone complained. The new BR red and cream livery has been applied with curious results to the leading coach, an LMS twin window third of 1926, while the 4LAV electric is still in Southern green.

Plate 12: One of the Class 2P rebuilt 4-4-0s with an assortment of stock heading south out of York on the East Coast Main Line in the summer of 1952. The white vehicle immediately behind No. 40480 is a refrigerated van with ice box cooling, while the rest of the train is LNER. These platforms were used occasionally for race and excursion traffic, which would have been in the way at the main York Station, hidden from our view by the girders of Leeman Road bridge. This train is bound for Sheffield, leaving the East Coast Main Line at Chaloner's Whin Junction, a mile or so ahead, so there won't be any need for fireworks from the 2P to keep out of the way of Gresley Pacifics.

Plate 13: The Midland habit of piloting died very hard, and well into the 1950s it was common to see express engines of a previous generation coupled ahead of their successors. On this occasion there seems to be some justification for it, because the 'Black Five' which is the train engine might have lost time with a 400 ton load on the Midland main line, something to be avoided on a summer Saturday if possible. The pair are making good speed on the four-track section near Elstree, in Hertfordshire, bound for St. Pancras with an express from Nottingham in 1958.

J.H.W. Kent

Plate 14: A glimpse into the past at Bedford Telegraph Office in November 1962. The 'counter' supported by a turned wooden leg carries four single needle telegraph instruments, and a sounder for the clerk to 'read' an incoming message by ear while he writes it down. There is another sounder on his desk, where modernity in the shape of a 1930s bakelite telephone intrudes into this vintage scene. The vases of flowers seem to suggest that there were lady clerks at Bedford Telegraph Office.

Plate 15: This Class 3F 0-6-0 was originally Somerset & Dorset Joint Railway No. 65, and was reboilered by Fowler just like its Midland brothers. It is just pulling out of Chesterfield goods early one morning in 1957, having shunted the yard and positioned the wagons ready for the day's work by the yard staff. On the right there is all the bustle of the start of the day — men hurrying about, trailers being shunted, and a general air of things getting under way. Both the old and the new varieties of mechanical horse, as the three-wheeled tractor units were officially called, are on view. Today they would be in the historic commercial vehicle class.

Plate 16: Despite the Midland policy of light trains run at frequent intervals, double-heading was common on the main line because of loading limits applied to the engines. This picture of the 'Thames Clyde Express' restarting from its Chesterfield stop shows Compound No. 41156 piloting the usual 'Jubilee' class 4-6-0. In 1957, the railways moved extensive coal traffic in wagons generally holding no more than 12 tons each, many of them still made of wood, and all requiring a vast provision of men, engines, and sidings. Unlike branch line closures or the end of steam traction, changes in the methods of handling this traffic have gone unrecorded by enthusiasts.

Plate 17: Yet more empty mineral wagons in east Derbyshire as a Class 4F 0-6-0 lifts a rake of empties over a hump on one of the colliery branches in the Staveley area. The 4F was the biggest Midland freight design. It dated from 1911 and, at a time when other companies with a large coal traffic had long been using eight-coupled engines, the LMS built hundreds more of the class. No.43869 is one of the Midland originals.

Plate 18: The Midland Counties Railway reached Nottingham in 1839 and this station saw its first passengers nine years later, although by 1961 only the site was the same. The GCR London Extension line crossed the Midland from 1898 to 1968 by the girder bridge in the background, and after five years of being upstaged by the newcomer's Victoria Station, the Midland opened this new station of its own, in 1904. BR named it Nottingham (Midland). The train is leaving the platform by one of the two scissors crossings which allowed each platform face to be used by two short trains.

Plate 19: A semi-fast train enters the east end of Nottingham (Midland) behind one of the many local Class 2P 4-4-0s, No. 40493. The GNR London Road (Low Level) Station was to the left of the Midland lines beyond the road bridge, while its high level lines passed close to the just visible gasholder in the distance, on their way up to the GCR Victoria Station.

Plate 20: This picture of Stamford Junction in Lincolnshire allows a comparison of the Midland and Great Northern styles of small signal box. It was taken in 1956 from the Midland line, looking towards Stamford (Town) which is round the corner to the left. On the right is the GNR signal box, controlling the exit from their station, Stamford (East), visible behind the train to Essendine. Even the insulators on the telegraph poles are different, although there actually are wires connecting the two boxes.

Plate 21: Although the Syston & Peterborough Railway was a company promoted by the Midland, the weathervane on its Stamford station proclaimed some sort of independence with the letters S&P. Class 2P No. 40485 was shedded at Leicester for working local trains over the line, and is homeward bound as it pulls away from Stamford (Town) in 1956. On the exteme right there is a very short MR signal controlling the exit from the bay platform, and below it, in the foreground, is one of the final pattern of Midland semaphore ground signals, designed by W.C. Acfield in 1919.

Plate 22: On a misty April morning in 1959, one of the last Johnson 0-4-4 tanks pushes the single coach from Rolleston Junction (on the Nottingham to Lincoln route) to Southwell, since 1929 the terminus for passenger trains on the line to Mansfield. The engine was built in 1892 but the carriage was only nine years old, although two months after this picture it had to find a new home when Southwell Station closed its doors to passengers.

Plate 23: Southwell Station's slightly gothic windows with standard MR diamond-shaped panes of glass fit in well with the church architecture for which the place is famous. In April 1959, the branch train to Rolleston Junction is seen ready to leave amid such authentic pre-grouping detail as the lower quadrant starting signal and one of the distinctive Midland platform barrows. The line beyond the crossing gates was goods only, to Mansfield. The Southwell branch remained faithful to Midland motive power to the end.

Plate 24: Before 1952 the first train of the day at Upton-on-Severn was a Malvern to Ashchurch local, but after the Malvern end closed to passengers they had to send an empty train out from Ashchurch to cater for Upton's commuters. It arrived in June 1961 behind Midland 0-6-0 No. 43754, with a single headlamp which proclaims it to be an empty wagon train. This offensive gesture foretold the complete withdrawal of passenger services three months later, although the goods continued to call for another two years.

Plate 25: A one coach train for a one station trip. Class 3F No. 43754 arrives at Tewkesbury after the 1¾ mile dash from Ashchurch (4 minutes allowed). Alas Tewkesbury's cluttered platform with all its Midland furniture closed two months after this picture was taken in June 1961. The square section telegraph pole with its fearsome spike finial (perhaps serving as a lightning conductor) is Midland, but the upper quadrant signals on GWR fittings are a strange product of nationalisation. Although it could be taken for brick, the station building is in fact made in local stone, as is the face of the platform.

Plate 26: The last Midland 'Belpaire ' (Class 3P 4-4-0) at Sheffield on a railtour to the Hull & Barnsley line in 1952. Built from 1900 to 1905, this class was S.W. Johnson's first advance towards the Class 4 Compounds, and the first with a Belpaire firebox, hence the nickname. The appearance of these engines had changed little since building, except for the tall Stanier chimney, pop valves, and an extended smokebox. How many people today remember that long lost hazard of the platform end, a water column 'bag' (hose) that leaked when the water was turned on, showering everbody within reach?

Plate 27: The leading wagons of this loose-coupled goods rattling through Matlock behind a Class 3F 0-6-0, display either a response to some very rough track — hardly likely on the main line to Manchester — or an urgent need of attention from the Carriage & Wagon Department. There is another of those massive square telegraph poles, but no spike, and one of the Midland's cast-iron 'rustic' seats on the platform.

Plate 28: Use of local building materials wherever possible was a tradition that the Midland shared with other enlightened companies, and apart from the carriages, some details on the engine, and the LMS sign for the 'Gents', this picture of Guiseley in 1955 could have been taken forty years before. However, there would not have been a Compound on the 2.12 p.m. Bradford (Forster Square) to Skipton, via Ilkley, and the porter would have been wearing his cap. Shed 20E was at Manningham, in Bradford.

Plate 29: A view from the fireman's side of Compound No. 41061 as it approaches Embsay on the line from Ilkley to Skipton. Today this same stretch of line is operated by the Yorkshire Dales Railway. The engine, like so many of its class, has acquired a Stanier chimney and an exhaust steam injector fed by the lagged pipe coming out of the base of the smokebox. The post and five-rail fence on the left is yet another Midland detail still in evidence in March 1955.

Plate 31: A goods train that starts with twenty or so loaded coal trucks and tails off out of sight might look more than a match for a 40 year old 0-6-0 locomotive, but the CLC line across the South Lancashire plain was almost level, and I suppose that once the crew of No. 43658 had got the train on the move they could keep it going without too much difficulty. Note the headcode − this is a through goods train, Class H. The signal box in the distance is Glazebrook West Junction, controlling the connection with the GCR lines to Wigan and St. Helens. Glazebrook's platforms are beyond the box, and the CLC line to Stockport goes off at the East Junction, beyond the station. In 1953 both these diverging lines still had passenger services.

Plate 30 (Left): Curiosity at Barnoldswick — a Midland Railway crossbar signal. When in the 'on' position, as shown, traffic in the goods yard was required to stop shunting, for it meant that the gates had been opened to road traffic. Interlocking was in the form of a chain attached to the crossing gate, which passed round a wheel fixed horizontally near the base of the signal post, and connected to the shaft on which the signal sits. When the gate was pushed closed, the 'crossbar' would swing round 90 degrees to face the road, indicating that it was safe to start shunting again. How much longer this relic survived I do not know, but Barnoldswick closed to goods traffic in 1966, ten years after this picture was taken.

Plate 32: When the Manchester Ship Canal was built in the 1890s, the CLC line between Irlam and Flixton had to be raised to pass over it. The catch points on the left will protect any train standing in Flixton Station behind the camera from a runaway back down the gradient. Compound No. 41188 from Aintree Shed is coasting downhill to stop at Flixton with the usual 1950s CLC mixture of LMS and LNER style carriages. Flat-bottomed rail has appeared on one track but the other is still bullhead.

Plate 33: The LMS built more 4-4-2 tanks for the LTSR section including No. 41952 (as No. 2134 in 1927) which passed into BR ownership. By 1953, when this picture was taken at Tilbury (Riverside), the GER, in the shape of the Eastern Region of BR, had finally obtained control, after being 'left at the altar' when the 'Tilbury' jilted it. Walter Hyde, the GER General Manager, lost his job for letting the bride run away with the Midland a rare example of such a senior officer actually getting the sack.

Plate 34: This fine pair of London, Tilbury & Southend Railway stop signals adorned the gantry at Barking. They had just been repainted in 1951 but must have disappeared long since. Only the taller signal has a ladder with bow, while the gantry itself, with steel plate stiffeners below the dolls, is unusual. It has blast deflecting shields above each track, very necessary in steam days, and diamond-shaped plates to indicate to enginemen that, while standing at the signals, their engine will be operating a track circuit in the signal box. This sign, now in universal use in this country, was another Midland Railway innovation.

Plate 35: The inter-war growth of oil imports provided the Tilbury section with a new traffic. Its pre-1939 shape can be seen from the second tank which is quite overshadowed by more modern vehicles at West Thurrock Junction in 1953. Certainly when Class 3F 0-6-2 tank No. 41985 was built by the North British Locomotive Works in Glasgow, in 1903, as No. 74 *Orsett*, its owners did not dream that it would spend its last years hauling oil trains, with just a little general traffic thrown in for light relief. The little ground signal in the foreground is also LTSR.

Plate 36: Tank engines were not turned after every trip on the 'Tilbury' as they were, for example, on the 'Brighton', so No. 41977 is working bunker first as is leaves Grays with an 'up' train in 1953. The very neat rake of carriages are Midland (see *Plate 37* for the 'Tilbury' outline) but the LMS fitted the Hudd ATC receiver below the engine's rear buffer beam in 1938. I think the figure 257 on the end of the nearest carriage is a set number; the design is the work of David Bain, who preceded Reid as head of the Carriage & Wagon side at Derby.

Plate 37: No. 80 *Thundersley*, restored after withdrawal, represents the final development of the LTSR 4-4-2 tank design which began in the 1880s. In 1956, the engine and the adjoining third class carriage were restored to near 'Tilbury' condition to celebrate the line's centenary, and worked several special trains including this one at Westcliff-on-Sea. *Thundersley* is owned by the National Railway Museum and is on loan to Bressingham Hall, at Diss in Norfolk. Sadly, the comfortable teak-bodied coach was broken up.

Plate 38: The branches from Upminster to Romford, and to Grays on the Barking to Tilbury line, were often worked by a three-coach push and pull train. Here, in front of 0-4-4 tank, No. 58054 (Derby 1892), it is entering the single line section at West Thurrock Junction. Only the fireman is on the engine and the driver is visible leaning out of the front coach to take the single line staff from the signalman. In 1953 one always regarded a branch line as an endangered species of railway life, but London's growth has ensured the survival of this one.

Plate 39: All LTSR tank engines were named after places in the district, although the Midland soon put a stop to such frivolity. No. 41983 was originally *Hadleigh.* As it stands at the outer end of Fenchurch Street Station (which was actually owned by the GER) we can see two details of 'Tilbury' design. The first is the heavy iron brackets sticking up from the buffer beam beside the normal lamp irons. They carried the front destination board which these engines, although a goods type, carried on days when East London made for Southend *en masse,* the Locomotive Department ran out of 4-4-2 tanks, and they were pressed into service. The other unusual detail is the massive guard irons bolted on to the face of the buffer beam. The 'Tilbury' was not taking any chances.

Plate 40: Although drivers on the Midland itself had to make do with 0-6-0s, Fowler designed some very modern 2-8-0s for the Somerset & Dorset Joint line in 1914. Boiler, cab and tender looked familiarly Midland, but marrying them to outside cylinders and Walschaerts valve gear was a new departure for Derby Works. In time they were clased as 7F; did anybody ever think of trying one on a coal train from Toton to Brent, I wonder? It might have avoided a lot of double-heading down the years. No. 53808 was one of the last built, in 1925 by Robert Stephenson & Co. In 1957 it was working a short goods into Evercreech Junction, and now it is preserved by the Somerset & Dorset Railway Museum Trust at the West Somerset Railway.

Plate 41: However much double-heading on the Midland main lines may have been the result of a 'small engine' policy over many years, on the Somerset & Dorset it was caused by the gradients. A ten-coach train would have been quite within the capabilities of a BR Standard Class 5 like No. 73051, but over the fierce grades north of Evercreech Junction a Class 2P pilot was a necessity if anything like time was to be kept. Here the pair are climbing the short double-track section from the S&D line at Templecombe to the 'Upper' or LSWR station. There was also a 'Lower' station, just a platform on the single line on the right which led to Blandford and Bournemouth. All this closed in 1966.

J.H.W. Kent

Plate 42: After nationalisation the Southern influence seemed to become stronger on the Somerset & Dorset Joint line and, for example, engine sheds were numbered in the Southern list, so Highbridge became 71J. Class 3F No. 43682, although drafted in from the London Midland Region, was similar to the local 0-6-0s, and therefore was immediately acceptable. Signalling on the Joint line had for many years been based on LSWR and SR designs, and the unusual 'backing' or 'reversing' signals, like the one on the right, probably derived from that fact.

Plate 43: Weston was the first station on the Midland Railway's Bath to Mangotsfield line, close enough to Bath for the gasholders to be visible. The engine on the coal train from Radstock in 1961 is one of the Class 7F 2-8-0s, with its tablet exchanger still projecting from the footplate, although it is on double track. It carries the normal mineral train headcode, which can be compared with the special code carried on the S&D by all goods trains, as in *Plate 40*.

Plate 44: A local train for Highbridge behind a Class 3F 0-6-0 which was built for the S&D, identical to the MR design, sets off from Evercreech Junction in 1954. Another engine of the same class stands at the opposite platform. The centre road was very useful on days when traffic was heavy, for in it the branch coaches could be stabled out of the way, yet easily accessible when the time came for a Highbridge train. Another use was to hold pilot engines waiting to help trains northbound over the step grades to Bath, long a feature of the working on Saturdays in the summer.

J.H.W. Kent

Plate 45: With a passenger train due very shortly, Class 7F No. 53808 was required to shunt its train of minerals into a siding at Shepton Mallet to clear the main line. In 1961, the little station, just visible in the distance, had only five years left before there were no more trains of any sort. Already the lineside allotment, once somebody's pride, is becoming neglected and overgrown.

Plate 46: What ghostly memories may have been around when this picture was taken in November 1961! Thirty two years before to the very day this same engine, Class 7F No. 53809, had stormed down the 1 in 50 and into Bath goods yard out of control with its driver dead on the footplate, gassed in Coombe Down Tunnel two miles to the south. It turned over, killing three railwaymen in a pile of wreckage immediately to the right of its position in this picture, where the shunting gong stands on its post.

It must be said at the outset that the London & North Western Railway presence on British Railways was very much less than that of the other large pre-grouping companies which made up the LMS. Only the Glasgow & South Western suffered a greater eclipse. It is inevitable that the presence (or absence) of locomotives designed before 1923 plays a large part in the assessment. In the 1950s, details of carriages and wagons were much less widely known than they are now, reinforcing the tendency to judge a railway's survival on the locomotive position. Even less information was available about the really detailed 'evidence' like signals or station furniture, neither had there been any detailed book on the LNWR since Steele's Edwardian history, long out of print. So the observer was left to look for the surviving signs of the old company wherever he might find them, with no guide of any kind to the 'remains' except the locomotive lists.

So far as those aspects of the LMS which the public in general and railway enthusiasts in particular noticed most, that is to say the trains, in England, at any rate, there had been something approaching a 'take over' by former Midland designs. In some ways excellent, they became the new standard. New equipment only began to have a distinctly LMS appearance in the 1930s. The first years of the LMS had a 'modified Midland' look about them, and the physical presence of the LNWR began to decrease from 1924 onwards. This decline was slow at first because the North Western did not bequeath a worn-out railway to the new owners, but it hastened with the years. The late 1940s, the first years of BR, marked the end of the time when LNWR objects were common on the Western Division, and in the 1950s engines, carriages, wagons, signals, and all the other things that the old company had produced became rarer and rarer.

In 1934 the headquarters of the LMS was concentrated in a new block of offices at Euston but, although it was intended, Euston Station was not replaced for another thirty years. As a result, just as for Londoners the Midland meant St. Pancras, so the LNWR meant Euston, the old Euston *(Plate 47)*. It is hard to do justice to its particular flavour. For a start, there never seemed to me to be any proper entrance. True we still had the Doric Arch, but once through that one did not follow an obvious route that led to booking office and trains. Originally the place had been well laid out, and it still preserved the logic of its origin, with separate parts of the station for departures (on the left, from the viewpoint of the intending passenger) and arrivals. The trouble was that the traffic would outgrow the facilities provided until, after congestion became unbearable, there would be an upheaval and new lines and platforms provided. When they too proved inadequate, there would be a further enlargement, but never a total clearance and replacement. The earliest of the additions came very early when, beside the departure area, they built the Great Hall and the adjoining Board and Shareholders' Rooms. Then there were platforms behind those, like No. 9 'The York'. Then there was an entirely new departure area outside that, and so it went on. The traveller and the visitor made of it what they could. World War II made the place shabbier, more ramshackle, and more confusing, not by bombing but by general neglect, although there were consolations. The historically-minded could wander round unchallenged — one could always claim to be lost, as people often were — and poke into little-used parts of the place that went back to its birth, but getting to the trains was another matter. About the last LNWR passenger engine duties in the London area were the Euston – Watford – Bletchley outer suburban trains, on which I just managed to see the last 'Prince of Wales' class 4-6-0s, but by 1950 they had all gone for scrap, along with every other North Western express engine, except *Hardwicke*. These Bletchley trains started from one of the intermediate platforms at Euston, tucked away behind the Great Hall between the arrival and departure

sections. The Watford electrics, still often LNWR stock, were there too. From the platform photography was difficult because the platforms had different lengths, one was always on the wrong one, and there was a bridge spanning the station throat. But in the end I came to like the old place because of its waywardness, and a picture of one of the older parts is included in this chapter.

Down the line from Euston in the earliest BR days one could still find LNWR engines at work, although they were not plentiful. Apart from the 0-8-0s, the remaining engines were almost, without exception, the work of F.W. Webb, rather than his successors. Down the years Webb has had a rough time from the commentators over his espousal of compounding and his fearsome autocratic ways which, it is alleged, kept from him the real state of the Motive Power Department. I think it is timely to point out that his simple engines, cheap to build and maintain, both performed and lasted very well, especially given the work exacted from them as a matter of course. Webb's successors Whale and Bowen Cooke needed only to weed out the Compounds, rather than replace the locomotive stock wholesale. Another point about Webb is that he was chosen by and served under Richard Moon, the Chairman who made the LNWR 'The Premier Line', and Moon was certainly not the man to allow inefficiency or waste to occur without visiting total penalty on the officer responsible. So Webb must have deserved his towering Victorian reputation, and his engines, which survived into BR days, were proof of it, unless, that is, Webb designed the Compounds and some unknown A.N. Other did the rest. All the delving and discoveries of British locomotive history have never come up with that idea.

I have already mentioned the 0-8-0s, and as there are numerous pictures of them in this chapter, a little of their history may be useful. They started as Webb Compounds in the 1890s, and rebuilding to Simples, reboilering, and new construction continued until 1922. Derby considered them satisfactory and LNWR enginemen regarded the superheated version as superb. Their history as a family was complex, but when the variation classed 'D' was superheated, the 'Super D' was created, and it was those which BR inherited. They lasted into the era of the West Coast Electrics, although by then they were often in poor shape, particularly as to their valve events. The characteristic sound of a 'Super D' on the move in the late 1950s was 'puff, PUFF, silence, HISS' *(Plate 54)*. However, their unusual appearance, and being the last LNWR class, made them worth seeking out, so I was prepared to leave home at a very early hour to spend a day with them at Nuneaton. Happily one is preserved, although not in working order. What a treat it would be to hear that unique noise again.

Another excursion to seek out remnants of the LNWR took me to the celebrated Cromford & High Peak line in Derbyshire, opened in 1830 as a horse and cable railway, and still partly worked by endless rope in the 1950s. Despite the shocking (to my railway-minded system) need to get a bus from Matlock to the foot of the first incline, it was worth it, because of the welcome that enthusiasts were sure of when visiting the line. I got off the bus near the bottom of the 1 in 9 Sheep Pasture Incline. A little way up its two tracks separated from one another for a distance, to go round a large pit which had been dug between them. Catch points on the incline tracks were controlled from a cabin nearby, and led directly into the hole, so any runaways could be diverted straight into the catch pit, as it was called. This precaution was necessary because the incline proper ended at a sharp curve where the C&HP met the Cromford Canal and the Midland main line and long ago, some runaway trucks had, it was said, reached such a speed that they had left the rails at the curve, jumped both the canal and the Midland Railway, and ended up on the banks of the River Derwent beyond. The catch pit effectively prevented a repetition of this performance, if indeed it was not just a tale.

Sheep Pasture Incline was about ¾ mile long, and an LNWR 2-4-0 tank nicknamed 'The Chopper' worked the ensuing mile of level — or rather it had done — but I arrived to find it had recently made a fatal visit to Crewe Works where it had been condemned. In its place to work the Sheep Pasture level stood No. 47000, an 0-4-0 saddle tank built for the LMS by Kitson & Co. in 1932, and on this I was invited to ride the mile or so to the foot of Middleton Incline. We set off, at no great speed through the woods, and the fireman casually opened the firehole door to see how things were in the firebox. The fire, he announced with a broad grin, had almost gone out while the engine was standing, and now showed no sign of life. There seemed to be no great concern about this as the boiler had enough steam for the run to Middleton, and working the engine a little harder against the brake would probably generate some life in the fire to raise steam for when it was wanted. Life on the High Peak line was delightfully relaxed that summer.

The C&HP ran for about fourteen miles across a waterless limestone upland, and one of the features of working it was the conveyance of water to the few houses connected with the railway, and for the steam engines, both locomotive and stationary. The water was carried in LNWR tenders, some of which looked to be of great age. The youngest were the wooden frame variety of Webb's years, built with the idea that the wooden frame tender would break up under impact, acting as a kind of shock absorber between train and engine if they ran into anything. There were also some plate-framed 4-wheelers which looked even older (Plate 70), and I was casually invited by the 'hooker-on' at Middleton Incline foot to ride up the incline on one of these ancients. Facing ½ mile of 1 in 8, I didn't need asking twice, and as I mounted the bank in style, the inclination caused water to spout from two valve spindle holes in the tank top. The fountains played as I rose up Middleton on an 1850s tender, hauled by an 1825 steam winding engine.

At the summit I duly paid my respects to the winding engine, and enquired after the train to Parsley Hay which I wanted to photograph coming up the 1 in 14 of Hopton Incline. 'Oh, the train's gone', they said, and as my face fell, 'If you hurry you'll catch him up at Hoptonwood — he'll be shunting at the quarry'. Walking along the sleepers is easy if you take your time and match your stride to them, but I had to run. I was nearing the portal of the short Hopton Tunnel when a train came through it and disappeared towards Middleton, which was disconcerting because I thought there was only one train. Pressing on through the tunnel at the run I came to the quarry branch junction to find the North London tank engine about to attack Hopton Incline, which looked an impossible climb. Breathless, I begged the driver to wait till I got to the top. 'Don't worry about that', he said, 'You can come up with us'. Facing great temptation I explained I wanted a picture of the train on the bank. 'Well you can do that too, 'cos we've got to make two trips to get this lot to the top', he explained. Even now I can hardly believe my luck. We backed towards the tunnel and then set off with a rush, the cut-off being progressively advanced to the full forward position when we were on the 1 in 14 incline. Years

Plate 47: Not merely the old Euston, but the original Euston, in October 1962, 125 years after opening. The first departure platform was now No. 6, although half its straight portion was swallowed up in later development so that the buffers were moved nearer Birmingham. On the left the slender iron columns supporting the roof trusses are the originals, elevated by the insertion of yard-long rectangular plinths. Finally, the pierced cast-iron arches on the right are either originals or copies of them; the design became an early LNWR standard.

before, some over-enthusiastic rushing of this bank had caused a derailment at the bottom and the engine ended in the nearby field, but today the old tank just settled down to its work, the load calculated to a nicety. And that was how the scene in *Plate 75* came to be photographed. You will believe that the rest of the day was an anticlimax.

Many of the pictures in this chapter have been contributed by others, because I did not visit the West Midlands where there were still quite a few LNWR tank engines at work at the beginning of the 1950s, neither did I ever travel over the renowned Cockermouth, Keswick & Penrith Railway in the days when all its trains were worked by Webb's 'Cauliflower' 0-6-0 goods engines. The Furness lines I also neglected, although, regarding the North Staffordshire territory, I can plead that BR had no NSR engines, and I had no idea what other North Staffordshire stock looked like. In extenuation of my failure to record other areas of the LNWR, I can also say that there was just so much pre-grouping equipment on the point of disappearance all over the country in the 1950s, and time and money were limited. Today I am indebted to kind friends who have allowed their pictures to be used, although I fear I can never repay the compliment.

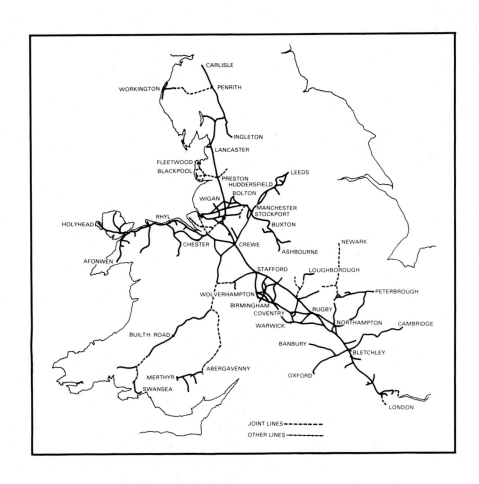

Plate 48: At the last only the 'Super D' 0-8-0s remained to remind us of the thousands of Crewe-built engines which had passed along these tracks at Willesden Junction. Somehow it seems appropriate that the train is a clanking and bumping collection of empty wooden coal wagons. In the early 1950s, when this picture was taken, North London still had trolleybus wires and gas street lamps.

J.H.W. Kent

Plate 49: The Dunstable branch train waits for customers in the side platforms at Leighton Buzzard, well clear of the thundering expresses on the main line. Compare the placing of the tool box in the bunker with the Midland practice of putting it on the footplate *(Plate 7)*, a matter of nuisance against accessibility. No. 58887 is one of F.W. Webb's 'Coal Tanks', at the end of its days fitted for pull and push working.

Lens of Sutton

Plate 50: An 'up' coal train bursts out of Northchurch Tunnel on the four track section of the LNWR main line between Tring and Berkhamsted in the summer of 1953. This picture allows close inspection of the Crewe smokebox door arrangements. Unkind commentators compared it to a dustbin lid but, although lacking the outwards dishing which was typical of most other builders' doors, to judge by the rarity of pictures of these engines with burned doors, it must have been very effective. This 'Super D' is No. 49430, shedded at Bletchley (2B).

OPC/Joint Venture

Plate 51: There was a time when every main shed on BR had a steam crane, kept ready with fire banked up, against the call to attend a derailment which could come at any moment, day or night. They were also used by the Civil Engineer for any heavy lifting jobs, so life wasn't all idleness. As engines, in particular, got heavier, cranes had to be replaced with more powerful specimens; I do not think many were ever scrapped because they were beyond economical repair. The LNWR remained faithful to hand-cranes long after many smaller railways had bought steam-powered outfits, but a change came in 1909, and this crane, from Cowans, Sheldon & Co. of Carlisle, was one of the first. It lasted long enough to have electrification flashes at Bletchley in 1962, and now it is preserved. The North Western knew how to get value for money.

Plate 52: As his engine restarts a heavy goods with the usual 0-8-0 noises, the fireman is still up on the tender shovelling some coal forward. Although there are electrification flashes on the boiler, in 1962, there is no sign of the wires that were to change the West Coast Main Line forever, but these water towers at Bletchley are not going to be needed very much longer.

Plate 53: This Wolverhampton to Walsall push and pull train has an excess of steam at the end of its journey, perhaps because the engine was a stranger from Warrington, and the fireman was used to a local 2-4-2 tank where he had to fight for every pound of pressure. At this moment of repose he is standing on the cab roof while the engine is refilled with water from a crane beneath Walsall's platform awning; quite an unusual position. For us the other novelty must be the siting of the engine's tank filler, in the middle of the coal bunker. Webb's LNWR tank engines had no 'piano front' (front fall-plate below the smokebox) so we can see the front of the large triangular steam chest which helped the 'Jumbo' 2-4-0s to such impressive downhill speeds. No. 46701 was long past trying to imitate them in 1952.

F.W. Shuttleworth

Plate 54: The steam leaking from the front end of this 'Super D' not only outlines its smokebox profile, but is a visual reminder of the typical LNWR 0-8-0 noise. This would be the 'HISS' phase of the cycle. The train of Engineer's hopper wagons is crossing over at the north end of Bletchley, on its way from some weekend works for the electrification of the West Coast Main Line, in 1962.

Plate 55: The 'Coal Engines' of 1873 were followed by 'Coal Tanks' from 1881. Three hundred were built, and once again the LNWR and its successors got value for their money. No. 58928 was still earning its keep as one of the station pilots at Birmingham (New Street) in 1950. Happily, one of these engines has been preserved to exemplify Crewe's 'cheap and cheerful' school of engine construction. Sneering competitors used to say LNWR locomotives were built of 'best cast iron and best lamp black'. The adjoining carriage is a corridor third, built for the Midland Railway about 1922.

F.W. Shuttleworth

Plate 56: The rare sight of a clean 0-8-0 (LNWR Class G2) at Nuneaton in 1959. The engine has just returned from Crewe Works with the second style of BR emblem on the tender which is fitted with a cab matching that on the engine. Among other details worth study are the LNWR type flat-faced driving wheel spokes of 'H' section, the flangeless third pair of wheels, and the neat reversing rod support bracket on top of the third splasher.

Plate 57: Photographed from the footbridge at the north end of Crewe Station, in August 1951, this front view of No. 58347 shows its normal duties, moving short rakes of goods wagons about the place. Shortly afterwards it was observed heading north on the goods lines underpass on the right of this picture, which allowed through freight trains to avoid fouling the junction with the Chester line at the north end of Crewe. These old Webb engines had his wooden-framed tenders, and skimpy cabs, thought to be sufficient protection in the 1870s. Above the tender there is the shape of the LNWR carriage profile of Webb's later years.

Plate 58: To judge from the condition of the paintwork, this picture and *Plate 57* must have been taken within a few days of each other. This one shows the cab scene of 'Coal Engine' No. 58347, one of several which were kept for strictly local work at Crewe in 1951. Despite its humble status, it has just been repainted, although not thought worthy of the new BR lion and wheel emblem. These tool boxes would have been easier to reach than those on the 'Coal Tank' in *Plate 49*.

R.J. Essery Collection

Plate 59: Even older than the 'Coal Engines' and 'Coal Tanks' were the 'Special Tanks' designed by Webb's predecessor at Crewe, John Ramsbottom, and built around 1870. A few survived into departmental use on BR including No. 3323, at Crewe Works. Appropriately it retained Ramsbottom safety-valves, but not his distinctive fluted-top chimney. By 1948 the old thing must have been getting pretty frail, but I cannot believe that the rope was to prevent the saddle tank blowing off in a high wind.

F.W. Shuttleworth

Plate 60: A 'Lanky Pug' far form home, at Devons Road Shed at Bow in East London. It is keeping company with a standard LMS 0-6-0 tank No. 47486, based on a Midland design (*see Plate 10*), and a North London railway 0-6-0 tank, No. 58858. As the L&Y handed over more of the 0-4-0 saddle tank type to the LMS than any other consitutent, their survival into the 1950s is not surprising. As well as dumb buffers it still has the sand shield over the crosshead and slidebars, with a bit of chain to hold it open when it is lifted by a driver wanting to oil the motion. The tool above the cylinder has a front-opening lid, but getting at the sand box next door must have been difficult.

J.H.W. Kent

Plate 61: The only North Staffordshire Railway steam engines to survive into BR days did not belong to British Railways at all, but to the National Coal Board at Walkden Colliery, in Lancashire. An 0-6-2 tank, *Princess,* was one of the NSR 'New L' class, built at Stoke in 1923 as the works plate proclaims. In 1952 it was still very much in NSR condition, and today it is preserved at Chatterley Whitfield Mining Museum in the Potteries.

Plate 62: The 'Great Ones' of British Railways still have official saloons but they cannot command a 2-4-2 tank to run them around their empire, neither have their vehicles the style of this clerestoried eight-wheeler. The engine is propelling along the line to Lees Station, and the white board on the upper lamp iron seems to be connected with this method of travel. In May 1953 there were still proper mills in this corner of Lancashire, and they were still driven by steam, as the smoking chimney indicates.

Jim Davenport

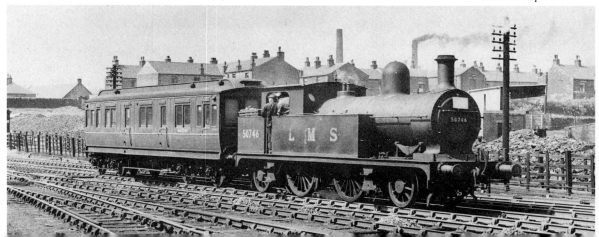

Plate 63: The 5ft. 6in. 2-4-2 tanks were a variation on the small-wheeled variety of the famous 'Jumbo' 2-4-0 tender engines, and far outlasted them. In 1952 No. 46604 was spending its last years as shed pilot at Bangor, in North Wales. It bears no indication of ownership, and the large numerals are thought to have been a transitional style in the early days of BR, this engine being renumbered in November 1948. I think the LNWR had its own brickworks tucked away somewhere on the system, because even in places like Bangor, where there was plenty of local stone, they did not use it for little buildings like the coalman's shelter. Maybe brick was cheaper.

Plate 64: The branch train from Delph in March 1955, just before the line closed, provided two LNWR carriages to add to the pre-grouping scene. The engine, an upper quadrant signal, and the signal box nameboard (Midland/LMS pattern) are about the only things not North Western in this picture. For the record, the two carriages are Nos. M3416 (Wolverton, 1911), nearer the camera, and M3427 of 1914. The single line to Delph is on the extreme left, with the train now on the main line.

Plate 66 (Below): A diminutive group of LNWR style signals was sited outside the back wall of the Oldham bay platform at Greenfield on the Manchester to Leeds line. The North Western was an early user of corrugated-metal signal arms, but the inner shunting signal still has a wooden one. The square flat cap became an LMS standard before wooden posts were abandoned in the 1930s.

Plate 65: The Manchester South Junction & Altrincham Joint Railway was shared with the GCR by the LNWR. It operated its own trains (with overhead wire electric traction from 1931) and also accommodated services of the Cheshire Lines Committee and the LNWR. The 'South Junction' of the title is with the former LNWR at London Road (now Piccadilly) Station, Manchester. The 7.57 a.m. Runcorn to London Road, via Ditton Junction and Timperley, train has just arrived behind 2-4-2 tank No. 50644 from Warrington Shed, giving passengers who hurry, a connection into the 'up' 'Mancunian', which leaves for Euston at 9.45 a.m. and is standing in the background.

Plate 67: As a contrast to the 'Special Tank' *(Plate 59)* the last LNWR tank engine design could only be called mammoth. They were the final development of the 0-8-0 goods type, for use on the steep gradients of the Abergavenny district. We can see the tank filler half-buried in the bunker coal, and there are lots of steps and handrails for firemen scaling the heights when it was time to take on more water. One other distinctive LNWR detail is also visible — the rounded bunker coal rails which the irreverent said were made out of old gas piping. No. 7954 was photographed at Buxton in August 1948.

F.W. Shuttleworth

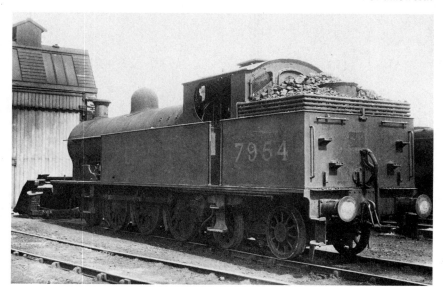

Plate 71 (Right): The one that got away — 2-4-0 tank No. 58092 was the last of the 'Chopper' tanks and survived in the mountains of the Peak District, working between the top of Sheep Pasture Incline and the bottom of Middleton, on the Cromford & High Peak line. In the last year of its activity, the traffic was the same as always — empty mineral wagons going up to the quarries, and filled water tanks for use on the dry limestone uplands which the line traversed. This engine was built at Crewe in 1877 and was scrapped in 1952.

R.J. Essery Collection

Plate 68: This scene of an LNWR 0-8-4 tank bustling along with a mixed loose-coupled goods in 1948 gives the opposite view from that in *Plate 67* — a top three-quarter showing the disposition of the boiler mountings. The limited coal and water capacity precluded this class from any long-distance work, despite the 'through goods' headcode which is being carried.

Lens of Sutton

Plate 69: It is no accident that so many pictures of trains in Lancashire contain, as part of the scenery, the brooding bulk of giant brick-built mills or warehouses like this one at Lees. The serried ranks of its windows look down on Class 3F No. 52248, as it stands in the sidings at the head of an excursion train laid on to take the trippers of Oldham to the seaside delights of Skegness, in June 1956. From Clegg Street Station, the route will be via Guide Bridge, where the 0-6-0 will hand over to an engine deemed more appropriate to the remainder of the journey.

Jim Davenport

Plate 70 (Right): Coming up Sheep Pasture Incline on the Cromford & High Peak line in 1953, an ordinary mineral wagon is accompanied by a very extraordinary vehicle, a mobile water tank. The latter may have been specially built for the job, but the plate frames and the arrangement of the springs are suspiciously like a Furness Railway tender built by Fairbairn's of Manchester in 1854 for attachment to a new 'Bury' type 0-4-0. If so, the footplate end is further from the camera.

Plate 72 (Below): Looking down Middleton Incline in 1953 some details of the equipment in use can be studied. The wire rope is continuous, being tied to the wagon's coupling. In the foreground the wooden blocks which are swung across the rails to stop wagons running over the edge of the incline are just visible, with a catch point beyond. It will be noticed that the track of the right-hand line is raised above that of the left-hand one. This is because it passes over a hump or 'kip' at the very top of the incline, which prevents loaded wagons which have just come up from running back down again if they recoil slightly as the ones at the bottom come to rest. That is why there are no stop blocks on the right-hand line, and why the short LNWR signal works only with the catch point on the left. Sometimes, however, wagons came up the left-hand line, despite these safety arrangements.

Plate 73: Several 0-6-0 tanks were transferred from the North London section to the Cromford & High Peak in 1931. No. 58850 was the first one built in 1879 and stands near the top of Middleton Incline in 1953, having recently been overhauled. The smokebox door with full-width hinges is unusual, and it carries the painted shedcode 17D, indicating Rowsley on the Midland line, two inclines and 700ft. below. Years later this engine found yet another home in the country, on the Bluebell Railway in Sussex.

Plate 74: Between the bottom of Hopton Incline (*Plate 75*) and the top of Middleton there was a short tunnel, seen behind the brake van on this train. North London tank No. 58850 has the usual load of mineral wagons and water tanks which are old Webb tenders this time. The home-made wooden 'cupboard door' which closed off part of the cab opening against the winter snows of the High Peak is not needed today, and is pushed back out of use until the summer is over.

Plate 75: There are no buildings in the wide-open spaces at the top of Hopton Incline for the thunderous exhaust of the North London tank to echo from, but the gradient board on the left says it all. This incline was originally worked by a stationary engine, but was turned over to locomotive haulage at some time in the past. I wonder who was the first brave driver to try it with his engine. At 1 in 14 it was the steepest adhesion-worked piece of standard gauge track in Britain, and this picture makes it appear that the gradient at the bottom was steeper than at the top. Note the odd arrangement of lamp irons on these North London tanks — four on the buffer beam, one on one side of the smokebox only, and one under the chimney. It was the same on the back of the cab, and a relic of their goods train days in North London.

Plate 76: The 'Cauliflower' 0-6-0s of the LNWR got their nickname from being enhanced with the company's coat of arms, which some wag said looked just like a cauliflower, and the name stuck. One of their last gathering places was on the Cockermouth, Keswick & Penrith line in Lakeland, where this picture of No. 58409 was taken. She stands outside the little shed at Penrith (12C) with a cab roof extension and the original wooden-framed tender which appears to have some sort of wooden cover on it, perhaps for snowplough duties. Unlike the 'Coal Engines' the 'Cauliflowers' often worked passenger trains, so they had conventionally-shaped spokes to their wheels.

R.J. Essery Collection

Plate 77: An earlier picture of No. 58409, this time in a proper Lakeland setting which those who know these noble mountains will surely be able to identify. The wooden tender cover is in place, and the engine has been renumbered in the transitional style with block numerals.

R.J. Essery Collection

Plate 78: Strangers would not expect the Oldham railway scene to be as leafy as this, but this train is in fact nearing Clegg Street Station. It is the 12.34 p.m. from Stockport (Edgeley) over the Oldham, Ashton & Guide Bridge GCR/LNWR Joint line. To add to the mixture we have an L&Y engine, standard 0-6-0 No. 52410 being the motive power in August 1957. This service through the south-eastern outskirts of Manchester was withdrawn in 1959, and another of those fascinating minor tables in Bradshaw was gone forever.

Jim Davenport

Plate 79: As well as a warehouse, Lees also had a station and an engine shed, 26F. The shed 'coal road' can just be seen on the right, while the station on the left is about to receive a call from the Delph to Oldham push and pull train (see Plate 64) in April 1953. I suspect that instead of putting a proper tail lamp on the engine at the rear of the train, the crew have 'made do' with leaving an engine headlamp in the 'stopping passenger' position. The engine is an ex-Lancashire & Yorkshire 2-4-2 tank.

Jim Davenport

Plate 80: Old and new at Lees Shed as L&Y 0-6-0 No. 52427 passes an LMS 2-6-4 tank standing in the shed yard. The train is the morning goods from Diggle on the LNWR Stalybridge to Leeds line, to Oldham (Glodwick Road), the LNWR outpost in Oldham. Traffic consists entirely of empty coal trucks, shepherded by No. 52427 which is actually passing its home shed. By July 1956 there were no passenger workings over this section, but the goods trains kept running until the end of 1963.

Jim Davenport

Plate 81: Like all the class this 'Super D' No. 49390 is innocent of any front numberplate. The obvious effort is directed to getting a heavy load of imported timber up the 1 in 33 of the Ribble Docks branch at Preston. As much of the climb from here on is in tunnel, we ought not to envy the crew the next few minutes.

Plate:82: Another glimpse of the West Coast Main Line in the days of steam and semaphores, this time at Preston. An LNWR 0-8-0 is passing one of the station's many signal boxes, this one built on a girder platform due to shortage of space between the Ribble Docks branch and the lines to Charles Street goods station situated behind the box. The engine is No. 49396, one of the last of the 'Super Ds', built in 1921, and seen here in August 1953.

Plate 83: British Railways inherited a few engines of the Furness Railway Class D5, and No. 52494, the only one still with a Furness boiler, was the oldest of them. In 1954 it was working the Moor Row to Millom goods near Wood End on the single track Whitehaven, Cleator & Egremont Joint line, which was local duty No. 99 and certainly not a hard task.

F.W. Shuttleworth

Plate 84: This close-up view of No. 52494, the last Furness Railway engine in anything near original condition, indicates that its local fame has led to the splasher beading getting a polish, as well as the North British Locomotive Company's 1913 works plate. The station in this 1954 picture is Egremont on the Furness/LNW Whitehaven, Cleator & Egremont Joint line. On the platform, just above the right-hand buffer, is one of the delightful FR platform seats with the cast-iron squirrel ends.

F.W. Shuttleworth

Plate 85 (Above): For comparison with the original version *(Plate 84)* this picture of one of the Furness Railway 0-6-0s, as rebuilt with a Lancashire & Yorkshire Railway Belpaire boiler, is included. Like the other Furness survivors it was based locally at Moor Row (12E) where this picture of it on a train of empty hopper wagons was taken. The leading one is of the NER wooden-bodied type, reminding us of the once extensive interchange of mineral traffic between Furness and Teeside, via Penrith and Barnard Castle. How suitable that in an ironworking district the footbridge staircase is a triumph of foundry art.

F.W. Shuttleworth

First impressions can be misleading, but my introduction to the Lancashire & Yorkshire Railway proved to be accurate. I had come over the Pennines from York by the LNWR route through Huddersfield and Standedge Tunnel, and as my train ran past Manchester (Victoria) into Exchange Station, there were two aspects of the 'Lanky' which turned out to be completely typical. It was pouring with rain and there was a line of Aspinall 0-6-0s waiting their turn on the banking duty at the east end of the station. The fearsome climb up the 'old road' to Miles Platting (Plate 86) seemed to claim most of their energies, although the more curved main line route past Red Bank carriage sidings looked fairly nasty too. The rain didn't help them or the train engines they were banking. I did later learn that it was not always raining in Manchester, and the 0-6-0s proved the longest lasting of L&Y engines. British Railways had inherited a large number of them in 1948 and, to a visitor from the south, they appeared to come in bewildering variety. There were long smokeboxes and short, round-topped boilers and Belpaires, and even some of the

older Barton Wright engines with rectangular panel cab-side sheets.

When I finally got my camera busy on th L&Y section it was exclusively in Lancashire, for which I apologise. My principal quarry was the famous 2-4-2 tanks which also came in several varieties. All this was before we had the detailed locomotive information which John Marshall's three volume history of the company made available. Eric Mason's work had introduced me to such legends as the 4.25 p.m. Salford to Colne train, first stop Burnley Barracks, and worked in its heroic days by a 2-4-2 tank, but by the 1950s such exploits were things of the past. Nevertheless, the fame of this class from former times, and the fact that they could still be seen and photographed, made me determined to seek them out. In those days, while local fanciers knew just where to look, outsiders like me had to rely on word of mouth. This was partly because such a famous class could still be seen daily, and didn't get much of a mention in enthusiasts' magazines. Eventually, when almost extinct, they had acquired a

Plate 86: First sight. The east end of Manchester (Victoria) Station leads immediately to severe gradients, and heavy trains going east were often banked, latterly by 0-6-0s which stood in a patient line on the multiple track section between platforms 11 and 12. This train has taken the stiffer climb, at 1 in 59/47 up to Miles Platting, by which the Manchester & Leeds Railway originally connected with pioneer Liverpool & Manchester Railway. For a short while the gradient was worked by a stationary engine and rope, but soon the locomotives were strong enough for the job. No. 52165 was built in 1892 as one of Aspinall's standard goods.

J.H.W. Kent

rarity value, but generally by that time, given the delay in reporting and publishing the news, when strangers did get to the scene it was too late. I do not remember the London Midland Region having the same fascination with a 'last of class' representative which, on the Southern, led to certain engines being kept going for months, or even years, after the rest of the class had been scrapped.

The word in the early 1950s was that the Bolton area was a good place to find the 2-4-2 tanks, there being several push and pull service workings using the ones shedded there. You can see from these pictures that the rumour was true, but I wish I had known of their other haunts. British Railways took over about ten different classes of L&Y engines, but some of these disappeared before 1952 when I first got to Lancashire, and others were only found in the depths of the local sheds. I am happy to record here my gratitude to the photographers who have allowed me to use the pictures which they, as local residents, were able to take. One long-forgotten problem that confronted us all, locals and visitors alike, was that, in the early days of BR, it was very difficult to buy film, and even if you became a regular customer of one shop you could still often be unable to get any film, let alone the brand or grade you wanted. If therefore some of these pre-1952 pictures are not of best quality, please blame the film shortage and not the photographers.

We all had our favourites among the pre-grouping classes of a particular company and, as far as the L&Y was concerned, the 2-4-2 or 'Radial' tanks were mine. Had I known them it might have been the large 0-8-0s which seem from these pictures to have had a most endearing confusion of appearance, with a very modern-looking large boiler and cab mounted on quite disproportionate-sized wheels *(Plate 100)*. However, among the types I did get to know, the 0-6-0 saddle tanks took a lot of beating for character. They looked a curiously antique design, the sort of thing that had flourished as shunting engines up to about 1900 before the side tank pattern of shunter became popular. They were, in fact, quite old, being conversions of the Barton Wright 0-6-0s mentioned earlier, which dated back to 1877. My efforts to find pictures of them at work rather than at rest have often elicited the response that that is what most people remembered, rarely being able to photograph them doing anything except 'just hanging around'. The truth I suppose, is that by the 1950s they did very little trip work and confined themselves to shunting, generally in

inaccessible places. The picture of one in company with a tar boiler at Preston was my only success in taking an 'action' picture *(Plate 93)*.

I have always thought it a pity that E. C. Trench, the LNWR officer who became Chief Civil Engineer of the new LMS, made such a nuisance of himself with the Chief Mechanical Engineer's Department in 1923 that George Hughes retired in his prime, rather than put up with any more of it. He had a fine design team at Horwich and they were within sight of success with the 4-6-0s. What, I wonder, would they have produced in place of Derby's 2Ps and Compounds, for secondary passenger services — some kind of shortened 'Dreadnought', an outside cylinder 4-4-0 perhaps? Imagine legions of Horwich 'Baltic' tanks instead of the Fowler 2-6-4 tanks. We shall never know. Of course, when it came, Stanier's 'new era' was so up to date that it stood the test of time and served as a basis for many of BR's standard engines, whereas Horwich's ideas might have stagnated through the 1930s, leaving the LMS in real trouble during World War II. I for one could have foregone the hundreds of Compounds, even though they perpetuated that great British classic, the large-wheeled passenger 4-4-0.

The former L&Y, which under the LMS became the Central Division, was a complex system, and I shall make no attempt to describe its lines or services. Anyway it has been done far better than I could by Eric Mason who knew every yard of it, and his book, *The Lancashire & Yorkshire Railway in the Twentieth Century*, has become a classic of its kind. More recent writers have treated us to detailed surveys of particular areas, like East Lancashire which seems to me somehow to be the L&Y heartland. It was the only area where they had no competition, and with a network of lines through those chimneyed and smoky valleys they kept intruders at bay. Even Midland imperialism couldn't get a foothold.

Before you look at the pictures let me draw your attention to two 'Lanky' specialities. One is the 18in. gauge steam works tramway at Horwich which survived long after the Crewe prototype had vanished *(Plate 109)* — the other is the endearing habit of retiring very old engines from the Barton Wright era to slippered ease as carriage warming plants, and of putting them by the station platforms where we could take pictures of them. Thank you very much.

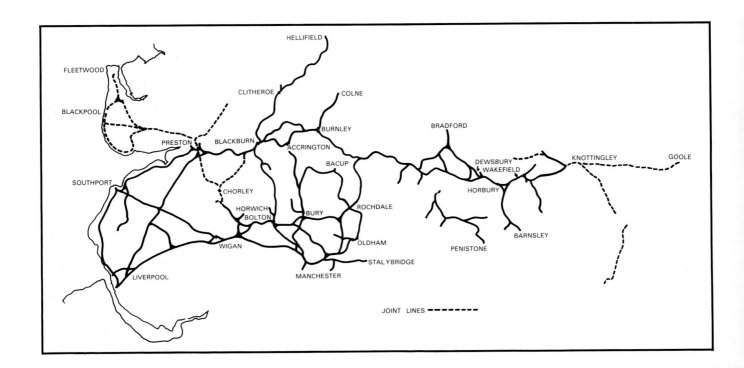

JOINT LINES ━ ━ ━ ━ ━

Plate 87: We should not be deceived by the sunshine in this picture. No. 52388 is pulling out of the 'up' yard at Royton Junction, near Oldham, which is over 600ft. up, and on the edge of the Pennines, and this is probably one of the rare days when shunting there isn't a penance. As well as the engine there is interest in the background of this view, which contains a common goods yard gas lamp, the outline of an 'Austin 7' (Fowler LMS Class 7F 0-8-0, very common hereabouts) and a water tower with two ladders, one for climbing up to it and another for climbing down inside.

Jim Davenport

Plate 88: The harsh reality of railway work in a northern winter is manifest in this view of saddle tank No. 51486 coming round the Jackson Street curve which joins the Preston and Blackburn lines at the north end of Bolton (Trinity Street) Station. In January 1960 there is plenty of snow on the ground, and more is falling heavily out of a leaden sky. It is what we used to call 'good shunting weather'.

Richard S. Greenwood

Plate 89: A 'Dreadnought' passing a Compound at St. Anne's in July 1950. With the first L&Y 4-6-0 appearing in 1908, just after *H.M.S. Dreadnought*, and eclipsing in point of size all other L&Y engines as the battleship had eclipsed all other warships, the origin of the nickname is obvious. Alas success did not follow, and it was not until 1920 that a revised and modernised version appeared. No. 10442 was built in 1923 by the LMS, but when George Hughes resigned in 1925, Fowler took over and the Compounds dominated new construction.

Frank Dean

Plate 90: The famous 2-4-2 tanks of the L&Y came in several varieties of smokebox, firebox, and bunker. No. 50660 of 1892, when photographed at Bolton July 1955, had none of the modifications which were introduced as the class multiplied. Livery apart, the changes from new seem to be the fitting of a Hughes-type smokebox door, pop valves, and vacuum-operated push and pull gear beside the smokebox. It has also lost one whistle and gained one coal rail. For comparison, facing it is one of the later extended smokebox engines.

Plate 91: One of Blackpool's L&Y standard 0-6-0s striding along beside the golf course on the line through Lytham and St. Anne's, in the early years of BR ownership. Over the years many engines built by Hughes' predecessors acquired his smokebox door, secured by edge dogs and lacking a handle. Instead it has a horizontal handrail with the upper lamp iron immediately above it, avoiding the need for short firemen to risk their necks trying to reach it. It also simplified the boiler handrail arrangements. Like many ex-L&Y engines having no smokebox numberplate in LMS days, No. 12447 will be given one by its new owners as soon as it is renumbered.

Lens of Sutton

Plate 92: In the days when Liverpool had both active docks and an Overhead Railway, the latter was called 'the dockers' umbrella'. In this early 1950s view 'The Pugs' umbrella' might be a better name. Putting the railway tracks connecting the docks under the LOR saved space, even though there might be some delay to road traffic when the shunter with his red flag appeared. In this picture the bus is turning away from a confrontation, and there is no tram in sight to dispute the right of way with the train as it crosses the tram lines.

R.J. Essery Collection

Plate 93: One of the Preston pilots, 0-6-0 saddle tank No. 51526, was converted from a Barton Wright tender engine in 1899, eighteen years after construction by Beyer Peacock & Co. In 1953 it had another four years life left. The unusual curved cab footsteps once matched a similar set on the tender *(see Plate 96)*, and the smokebox retains its old pattern door, unlike so many which were given the Hughes pattern with dog clips. On the right we can see into the gloom of Butler Street goods station which was exclusively LYR, as were the former East Lancashire Railway platforms of the passenger station just appearing on the left. The ancestry of the tar boiler is unknown.

Plate 94: The tenders of late Victorian Lancashire & Yorkshire engines look quite normal from the front, but viewed from behind the centre line they can be seen to have a slightly odd appearance, which is not an optical illusion. They actually were higher at the back than the front — not by much, but just enough to make the coal rails slope downhill towards the cab. Aspinall 0-6-0 No. 52427 is doing a little gentle shunting beside Waterloo Sidings signal box at Oldham (Clegg Street), with an array of short-arm shunting signals and a giant cotton mill to add to the scenery in 1955.

Plate 95: Very few of the 2-4-2 tanks which carried superheated boilers survived their energetic performances long enough to become BR property, so No. 50887 with Belpaire boiler, extended smokebox and long bunker, being almost identical in appearance, must stand in for the departed in this review of L&Y classes at work. It is the station pilot at Bolton, attaching some vans to the rear of a train to Wigan and Liverpool in 1953. They present quite a contrast in roof-lines, the six-wheeler further from the camera being designed to take objects of large dimensions, perhaps stage scenery.

Plate 96: The Victorian fashion for rectangular cab side-sheets appeared in Barton Wright's 1877 0-6-0s, although, as this sunlit picture shows, the part ahead of the cab frontplate enclosed nothing. All the original engines of this class were rebuilt to the 0-6-0 saddle tank design by Aspinall, before he produced his own standard 0-6-0s he bought 50 more of the previous design from outside builders. No. 52021 came from the Vulcan Foundry at Newton-le-Willows in 1887, and was still working from Springs Branch Shed, at Wigan, in 1953. It had the Barton Wright design of tender with a sharply projecting coping, no coal rails, and the plate frames cut in a regular curve from one axlebox to the next, which became an L&Y feature.

Photomatic

Plate 97: The Aspinall standard 0-6-0s began to appear less than two years after the last of the Barton Wright design was delivered, and the similarity in appearance is obvious. However, the new engines had larger wheels and were more at home on passenger work, although when No. 52099 was sent to the 'Western Front' in France in 1917, it would have done little express running. The hole in the buffer beam between the buffer and the coupling was for fixing the side chains which were thought necessary on French rails. It returned safely in 1919 and survived to work the Lees Shed tool van in 1953, which was an L&Y 'birdcage' six-wheeled brake.

Jim Davenport

Plate 98: The five miles of quadruple track south of Preston on the West Coast Main Line was LNW/LY joint property, so No. 52619 would not have been trespassing even before the Grouping. In May 1950 it was heading a procession of coal wagons, scarcely any of them built of steel, and we must hope that their axleboxes could cope with the speed needed to keep out of the way of main line expresses as they rattled south from Farington. At least they are in charge of one of the superheated rebuilds of Aspinall's standard goods engines, which should ensure a satisfactory rate of progress.

R.J. Essery Collection

Plate 99: The dawn of this century found the L&Y handling more and more coal traffic and needing engines with more simple brute strength than the Aspinall 0-6-0s, good though they were. As on the LNWR, the answer was an 0-8-0 design, robust and straightforward. Although Aspinall's successor, H.A. Hoy, experimented with compounding and fancy fireboxes, the only real development of the original 0-8-0s was the fitting of larger boilers by Hughes. No 52727 retained its original small boiler until the end which came in October 1950. This picture was taken then, at Horwich, when it was the sole survivor of the class. It has the eight-wheeled tender with double elliptical springs, designed by Hoy in 1902.

Photomatic

Plate 100: Pictures of the L&Y 0-8-0s at work in BR days are scarce, because the last one was withdrawn in 1951. No. 52857 was one of the large boiler variety, built in 1913 and later fitted with a Hughes' side window cab, increasing the impression that there ought to be some more wheels somewhere, to support such a load. Unhappily the bearing surfaces were also inadequate for the great power generated, hastening the demise of this class. The engine is on the LNWR line at Wigan with a goods train from the L&Y Wallgate Station.

Frank Dean

Plate 101: Running excursions to Blackpool is all very well, but having to pilot a large-wheeled express engine like BR Pacific No. 72003 *Clan Fraser* must have put quite a strain on L&Y 0-6-0 No. 52410, although the length of the train justifies assistance. It is a very heavy 9.30 a.m. Manchester (Victoria) to Glasgow and Edinburgh, on 14th July 1955, which might cause delay to other trains on a busy Saturday if left to tackle the long climb to Lostock Junction unaided. The 0-6-0 will come off at Preston, but here the pair have just cleared Agecroft Junction, 3¼ miles out of Victoria.

Jim Davenport

Plate 102: Midland engines found their way on to the L&Y section, 4F Class 0-6-0 No. 43893 being shedded at Lower Darwen (24D) in 1962. This wintry picture shows it passing Smithy Bridge on the main Lancashire & Yorkshire Trans-Pennine route just before Christmas of that year, with a train of coal empties.

Richard S. Greenwood

Plate 103: A Colne to Blackpool (Central) train approaches Wrea Green on the Lytham line in 1948. The engine is the last of the original batch of Hughes 4-6-0s to remain in service, No. 10412 dating from 1908, although rebuilt with new cylinders and motion, etc. in 1921, when superheating was also installed. As these 4-6-0s were not standard with Stanier types, even the engines built new with these modifications did not last much longer. The sharply curved line coming in from the left is the original route from Kirkham to Wrea Green, reduced to the status of a siding in 1874 when the direct line from Kirkham was opened. The run of the point rodding to the catch point is unusually agricultural.

Frank Dean

Plate 104: The location of this picture could not be in any doubt, even without a station nameboard. The L&Y named it 'Central', and so it remained until it was closed in 1964 by BR who sold it to become a bingo hall and car-park. Blackpool (South), formerly Waterloo Road, took over its duties, but not before the last 'Dreadnought' made a farewell run to York on 1st July 1951. No. 50455 was the first of the 1924 batch, shedded at Blackpool, and broken up soon after its final fling. In the background is the 'new order' in the shape of Class 2MT 2-6-0 No. 46412.

Frank Dean

Plate 105: These relics of the past warmed the carriages in winter for two whole generations of Blackpool passengers from Central Station. They are Barton Wright 0-4-4 tanks, built between 1877 and 1886, withdrawn from active service long before the Grouping, and finally scrapped about 1964. The motion and driving wheels have been removed, but the other wheels were used to tow them to Horwich when their boilers needed major attention. Nobody seems to have a picture of such an unusual movement, which would have been by goods train, nor is there any certainty exactly which two members of the class these are. It appears from the curved bracket on the smokebox that they carried their extension chimneys with them when on the move. At Blackpool, in 1951, they were firmly anchored by steam pipes, and dirt.

Plate 106: Although one always thinks of Blackpool as served only by the L&Y, the railways there were all owned by the Preston & Wyre Joint Committee, in which the LNWR had a one third share. There were three stations at Blackpool, the 'North' being called Talbot Road for many years. As well as the establishment with an all-over roof, seen behind the pilot engine, 0-6-0 No. 52523, there were excursion platforms, greater in extent and quite open to the weather. The engine shown in this 1958 view was one of several of Hughes' piston-valve superheated 0-6-0s which were 'downgraded' by receiving saturated round-topped boilers and slide-valves, although retaining the long front sand boxes which now project beyond the smokebox door.

Frank Dean

Plate 107: One of Blackpool's remaining 'Dreadnoughts', much reduced in circumstances, approaches Kirkham North Junction with a short goods and coal train in August 1949. The signal box in the background played a key part in working this complex three-way junction. Behind the brake van the lines go left for Blackpool via Lytham, straight on for Blackpool direct (the Marton line, closed in 1967), and to Poulton. Lastly, and directly in front of the box, we can see the single line connection from the flyover by which 'up' Marton line trains avoided fouling the Poulton line. Imagine this layout in the 1950s, with trains on a Saturday passing at one a minute for hours on end. Things were quieter when No. 10442 loafed in from St. Anne's Yard, and running tender first allows us to see the distinctive flat-topped roof of the Hughes cab.

Frank Dean

Plate 108: Bradkirk signal box from which this picture was taken stood between the line from Kirkham to Poulton and Fleetwood (on the left) and the direct Kirkham to Blackpool (Central) line, diverging out of sight on the right. This train is running Class E with the vacuum brake in use on the leading Conflats. The engine doing its best to soil the white paintwork is an Aspinall 0-6-0, given a Belpaire boiler by Hughes, and making good use of it in June 1957 as it roars with a Ribble Sidings (Preston) to Wyre Dock goods.

Frank Dean

Plate 109: By 1952 the chief delight at Horwich Works was the 18in. gauge tramway that still possessed one of the steam engines, *Wren*, which with its tender weighed 3¾ tons. At one time there were seven others, of which it is recorded that when they suffered derailment on the rough track around and about the Works, brawny workmen picked them up and put them on the rails again. Crewe Works pioneered the narrow gauge Works tramway, but that disappeared between the wars. Today *Wren* is owned by the National Railway Museum.

Plate 110: Although a small town existed at Horwich before the L&Y built its Locomotive Works there, that action trebled its population, and by selling surplus land the railway obtained its new establishment very cheaply indeed. It is on the western edge of the Pennines which rise behind the train leaving for Blackrod, the junction with the Bolton to Chorley line. Before it closed in 1966 there was also the usual goods and coal yard on either side of the single platform. Horwich Works is situated on the right of the running line, some distance behind the camera. The push and pull train, on 30th July 1955, is being worked by 2-4-2 tank No. 50731, which had been rebuilt with a Belpaire firebox and extended smokebox.

Plate 111: Spark arrestors have disfigured many an engine by making the chimney top grotesque, but the device used on the L&Y Class 24 0-6-0 side tanks beggars description. It obviously could be swung round over the chimney, when it would appear to act more as a blast deflector than anything else, and presumably deflected the sparks downwards instead of showering them far and wide. It was part of the equipment for working in Liverpool's dockland, like the flangeless centre driving wheels. No. 51537 outlasted all other members of its class, until 1961. At Aintree Shed, in 1958, it still had its L&Y class number displayed at the top of the cab side sheet, which also proclaimed it BR Class 1F.

Photomatic

Plate 112: Allowed out on the running line for once, 0-6-0 saddle tank No. 51458 departs from Royton Junction Yard with a short freight train. The empty state of the coal bunker seems to indicate that this is the end of a long day's shunting in the Oldham area, and the fireman is reaching through the open cab window with his shovel to try to scrape some coal down to the shovel plate. Unlike a side tank engine, saddle tank types have no obvious place to keep fire irons and here they have been carefully provided with a bracket on the back of the bunker, just above the left buffer. Experience presumably showed that they did not fall off, but it seems rather a precarious place all the same. They certainly would not be obtainable while on the move.

Jim Davenport

Plate 113: The Bury to Holcombe Brook branch enjoyed two different types of electric traction before reverting to steam haulage for its last year of passenger operation. The first was of the overhead wire sort with portal gantries, superseded after five years by a third rail side contact system with protective boarding. It can be seen on the left, in front of the engine, as it nears Woolfold on the last day of operation, 5th May 1952. With traffic declining on the branch it was not worth renewing when worn out by 1951. 2-4-2 tank, No. 50651, like all the push and pull engines, has two vacuum standpipes on the buffer beam, one for the brake (left) and the other for controlling the regulator by the equipment on the footplating and smokebox.

Jim Davenport

Plate 114: Someone has been polishing the dome of this Aspinall 0-6-0 (L&Y Class 27, LMS Class 3F) so it must have been good for a day's work in July 1956, aged 55 years. Like the wooden coal wagons it was not to remain active for much longer, being scrapped in 1958. If you find the shape of the chimney top somehow familiar, it is because by some strange chance its curvature was copied for British Railways' standard engines.

Jim Davenport

Plate 115: Amid a confusion of mechanical horses, L&Y 'Pug' tank No. 51207 shunts at Irwell Street goods station, in Salford, part of which was on the site of the New Bailey prison, closed in 1868. As it was at canal level this station was originally reached by a wagon hoist from the running lines up on the viaduct, but a 1 in 27 incline was opened in 1877 up and down, which shunting engines had to work until the whole complex was closed in 1967. In some of the sharply curved sidings only short wheelbase engines like No. 51207 could be used.

Richard S. Greenwood

Plate 116: The bottom of the 1 in 27 incline down to Irwell Street goods station is on the extreme left beyond the viaduct carrying the LNWR line from Liverpool into Manchester (Exchange). The saddle tank is No. 51496 with fire irons on the rear buffer beam, as usual. There will be trouble in due course for whoever loaded the 'B' container in an open wagon rather than on a Conflat, for few goods yard cranes could lift high enough to get a container out again over the side of the wagon.

Richard S. Greenwood

Plate 117: The Bolton – Bury – Rochdale local service was provided with a post-war motor driving trailer compared with others pictured, and this view shows it on an evening working arriving at Bradley Fold in August 1953, pushed by 2-4-2 tank No. 50731. This local service managed to keep going (although not with 2-4-2 tanks) until 1970. Details worth noting on the coach end are the warning horn projecting above the driver's window, and the abbreviation 'Pl & Ph' as a painted description of the vehicle.

Plate 118: Another view of the Bolton to Rochdale motor train, emerging from its siding by Trinity Street Station at Bolton, to take up a working to Rochdale. The 2-4-2 tank, No. 50731, was built in 1896 with a round-topped boiler, and rebuilt as shown in 1912. Long bunkers for this class did not appear until the end of 1898.

Plate 119: A very typical station scene in steam days, set at Bolton (Trinity Street). The pilot, 2-4-2 tank No. 50887, stands quietly simmering at the platform in one of the intervals between trains, and the staff who have been loading packages into a van under the eye of the Station Inspector are joined for a moment by a pair of enginemen, who no doubt pass jocular remarks about having a dry and comfortable job without too much to do. It is just a passing moment in the life of the station, yet I think it captures the flavour of life on the railway in the 1950s, before the great changes which were on the horizon.

Plate 120: Until the 1950s large quantities of freight were moved by the railways in odd wagon loads, each making its way to its destination by a series of short trips from one local shunting yard to another. Eventually they might form part of the load of a long-distance train, which would improve their average speed quite a lot, but then at the other end of the journey there would be another series of trips to the final destination. It all took days rather than hours, but it did provide photographers with lots of goods trains to record, like this Hollinwood to Moston working, in July 1952. It is passing the explicitly-named Vitriol Works Sidings at Middleton Junction. Behind the 0-6-0 there is every sort of wagon, probably going to as many destinations.

Jim Davenport

Plate 121: The growth of traffic through Preston caused a complicated set of curves and junctions to be made south of the station, which allowed many different routeings. The more contorted were generally with the aim of minimising movements across the West Coast Main Line on the level. The goods crossing over the quadruple tracks at Farington has come from Butler Street goods station which actually adjoins the passenger station *(see Plate 93)*, and is going to Ribble Sidings on the other side of the main line about ¼ mile distant. To get there without causing delay to express traffic means a five-mile transfer trip behind 0-6-0 saddle tank No. 11345. In 1948, Farington Station is still largely in LNWR condition, including the characteristic pavement blocks, nameboard, and gaslamp with an advertisement hung upon it.
Frank Dean

Plate 122: The 'Colne Motor' provided an 'all stations' service between Colne and Burnley to compete with the electric trams, but even extending it to Rose Grove and giving better onward connections failed to hold back the buses, and road transport won in the end. By July 1955 the 'motor' was a 2-4-2 tank working push and pull with two coaches, the leading one a 1938 conversion of an early LMS vehicle. It was given a centre entrance and vacuum-operated steps for low platform halts. The engine is No. 50653, with round-topped boiler and a short bunker which has acquired no less than seven coal rails. Today Rose Grove is served by diesel multiple units and there is no 'motor' waiting in the bay.

Plate 123: Unlike Shaw (*Plate 125*) Bacup has lost its trains, in 1966 to be exact. At one time you could arrive there from Rochdale on the L&Y main line across the Pennines, or as this train is doing, from Bury on the Accrington line. Either way it was a tremendous climb and behind the train we can see the beginning of the 1 in 65 down to Stubbins Junction. The Rochdale line was even worse, climbing out of Bacup at 1 in 34 before dropping almost as steeply all the way to near Rochdale, but that mountainous route closed in 1947. A 2-4-2 tank, No. 50829, one of the Belpaire long-bunker variety, was based at Bacup's little shed (26E) in August 1953.

Jim Davenport

Plate 124: The end of a June day was about the only time in the year that the 8.35 p.m. Royton Junction to Brewery Sidings trip could be photographed, for it was normally a creature of the dark hours. The Royton pilot, an unidentified 0-6-0 saddle tank, is in charge of the trip, and seems to be making a determined effort to get home.

Brian Hilton

Plate 125: Coal, steam power, and the cotton trade were the making of Oldham, Rochdale, and the district between. The Aspinall 0-6-0, No. 52410 which is shunting coal wagons at Shaw & Crompton' must stand for the first two influences, while the great cotton mills almost speak for themselves. The confidence they once displayed is waning in June 1956, their chimneys are smokeless, and there certainly will not be the lights of a night shift after dark. Now the goods engine has little shunting to do, although the starting signal for Shaw Station in the background is 'off' for a Rochdale train. In 1986 the station is still open.

Jim Davenport

Plate 126: The last run of the last 'Dreadnought' makes a **proper conclusion to the** Lancashire & Yorkshire chapter. No. 50455 was well-groomed but not, alas, in good fettle for the trip from Blackpool to York and back, running hot on the return journey. Nevertheless the outing was enjoyed by everybody who took part, although it provided photographers with the usual dilemma — to travel or take pictures.

R.J. Essery Collection

However much dispute there may have been among enthusiasts in Scotland about the fact, I think most railway visitors from England, if asked, would have acknowledged the Caledonian as Scotland's foremost railway. The acknowledgement might have been somewhat offhand if they were fanciers of the East Coast route, and therefore regarded the North British Railway as the company which came first to mind when considering Scottish railway affairs. Nevertheless, most interested people supposed, and some knew for certain, that the Caledonian was pre-eminent. This superiority was not based on seniority, because both CR and NBR could claim some very early railway ancestors. Rather, I think, it was because, over many years, the Caledonian had a way of doing things which other and lesser companies came to follow.

There is no doubt that the blue locomotive livery, which those who can remember it make so much of, played its part, but there must have been more to the Caledonian's leading position than that. There was the fact that the standard of locomotive work in the late Victorian and Edwardian period far surpassed the performance of any other Scottish company, thanks to the designs of J.F. McIntosh and his leadership of his department. Another thing that helped was the almost opulent way the railway renewed some of its more prominent assets in those years of prosperity. Yet with all the splendours of, for example, the new Glasgow (Central) station, there was also Buchanan St. Station on the other side of town, Glasgow's most ramshackle terminus. That belonged to the same Caledonian Railway.

After the Grouping, the LMS spent quite heavily on new rolling stock for the Caledonian section, which had the least need of it, although in the end the GSWR and the Highland did get a look in, and became almost totally LMS as their worn-out equipment was ruthlessly scrapped. By the 1950s, when one was considering how much survived from before 1923, the comparison was not so much with the other Scottish parts of the LMS, as with the North British section of the LNER. In the end the honours were about even, because both companies' engines lasted in similar numbers to about the same date, the early 1960s, and perhaps ex-NBR carriages were slightly more plentiful in the 1950s.

It is fitting that this ultimate comparison should have been between two old enemies, for the NBR spent much of its life trying either to keep up with the Caledonian, or catch up with it when it forged ahead. The story of the NBR's desparate response to the 'Grampian Corridor' trains of 1905, and how it tripped over its own feet, has been told elsewhere, and the episode seems typical of the relationship between the two companies. The North British was certainly a worthy enterprise, but instead of ignoring its rival, it seems to have been mesmerised into a kind of inferiority complex. This may be less than fair, but the fact remains that the Caledonian was 'top dog', and it wasn't only carrying the old Queen to Balmoral for so many years, or appropriating the Scottish Royal coat of arms for itself, that made it so.

In the 1950s, English railway enthusiasts going north to sample the CR did not get much of a taste of it at Carlisle, where the standardised LMS influence was very strong. My first sense of being in Caledonian territory always came at Beattock. If the train stopped there to take a banker to the summit, there would be CR 0-4-4 tanks and perhaps some 0-6-0 goods, standing at the shed, and even if the train didn't stop, there would be glimpses of them as we rushed by. Gradually, as the enjoyable scenery of the Tinto and the upper Clyde Valley gave way to the industrial approaches to Glasgow, more and more Caledonian Railway engines and other features would be seen. Unlike the East Coast approach to Edinburgh, the West Coast approach to Glasgow was a steady build up of railway interest, an increasing number of lines and yards to be seen, each providing glimpses of pre-grouping steam at work. The high point was the run in across the Clyde Bridge to

Central Station, which is captured in one of these pictures (Plate 147). Fittingly, some of the station pilots at Glasgow (Central) were CR 0-4-4 tanks, almost to the last days of that class.

The Caledonian Railway presence in Glasgow was virtually all-embracing, although in the south-western sector it was by virtue of partnership in lines joint with the GSWR. As well as all round the city, the railway went under it, with the completion in the 1890s of the Glasgow Central Railway, which gave a direct connection between the areas of heavy industry south and east of the city, and the docks and shipyards on the north bank of the river downstream from Central Station. Providing a through route for goods traffic was by no means the only reason for the underground line. As the NBR had found when they opened a similar route some years earlier, it generated short-distance passenger traffic, and relieved their main line of the suburban trains. Despite electric trams in the twentieth century (was it a Glaswegian who lyrically described them as 'the gondolas of the people'?) the lines of both companies kept their traffic long enough to be still in use when railway electrification reached Glasgow. But they have lost their inimitable character with the disappearance of steam traction, although I am sure the passengers are glad of the change.

However sharp the inter-company competition was in Glasgow, there was no denying that the NBR was supreme in Edinburgh, and indeed until it opened the new Princes St. Station in 1894, the Caledonian Railway made a poor showing in the Scottish capital. That is not to say that the old Waverley Station was anything for the opposition to be proud of, but the CR had no route through the city, and the NBR was left in undisturbed possession of Haddingtonshire. There was some competition for traffic associated with the docks at Granton and Leith, but the NBR dominated the services to England, and had the better route to Glasgow, and to the north via the Forth Bridge. The population of the Edinburgh district was much smaller than that of Clydeside, and there was by comparison little suburban or industrial traffic, so perhaps a subordinate position did not unduly worry the Caledonian Railway Directors.

However modest their company's presence in Edinburgh was before the Grouping, it has now suffered almost total eclipse. My last visit to the city was a winter one, but still I went to pay my respects to Princes St. Station, and in so doing received a nasty shock, for where once there were 0-4-4 tanks on the 'Leiths' and 'Balernos', there was only a heap of stone blocks in ruins all around — the whole station had been demolished. I came away quickly, for although there are no pictures of it in this book, I had happy memories of that station, and saw my first 'Dunalastair' there.

The oldest engines in these pictures are the work of Dugald Drummond, who arrived on the CR in 1882, having previously been in charge of NBR locomotives since he gave up his position as Works Manager at Brighton under William Stroudley. In 1891 he was succeeded briefly by Hugh Smellie who died soon afterwards, and John Lambie took over until 1895. On his retirement the Board appointed John Farquharson McIntosh, who had been Lambie's assistant, and it was he who led the CR locomotive department to its greatest achievements, especially by the evolution of the 4-4-0s, between 1896 and 1910, when the first superheated 'Dunalastair IV' was built. There is a picture of it in Plate 153. In turn, the 4-4-0s were succeeded on the heaviest trains by 4-6-0s, which were all scrapped before the last war. When McIntosh retired in 1914, William Pickersgill of the Great North of Scotland Railway was appointed, and there was a certain change in direction of Caledonian Railway locomotive affairs. Outside cylinders made a reappearance, notably on the '60' class, but Pickersgill's original designs were not, alas, improvements on their predecessors, and in the final years before the Grouping, the CR was still rather basking in a glory that had departed with McIntosh. However, the quality of design and construction ensured that there were still plenty of CR engines to be seen in the 1950s, for which many photographers and enthusiasts were very grateful.

I first came to Scotland with a camera just in time to photograph McIntosh's last development of the 'Dunalastair' design, the 'Dunalastair IV Superheater', while similar engines by Pickersgill were quite widespread, and lasted into the 1960s. They had little or no express work by then, although the picture *(Plate 128)* of a 'Pickersgill' on a Lanarkshire business train has quite an 'express' air about it. On the Highland section, and on the GSWR section Clyde Coast services out of St. Enoch, they were quite common on stopping trains. It was rather surprising to find one on a North British service, but that was the result of one engine shed at Perth being responsible for all duties.

The 0-4-4 tanks also spread their activities into other areas of the LMS in Scotland and, after nationalisation, to former LNER lines as well. I have included pictures taken on the latter in the Caledonian part of this book, but views of them working on the former HR and GSWR are grouped together with other designs seen on those sections in the 1950s. The 0-4-4 tank was a development of Stroudley's 0-4-2 tank design for the LBSCR, primarily through the agency of Drummond, and the same could be said of the 0-6-0 tender engines. Drummond's first 'Jumbos' of 1883 were very similar to those built by Stroudley at Brighton, and

subsequent development and enlargement of the type continued almost to the end of the Caledonian Railway's independent existance. They too were to be found on the HR and the GSWR, following the scrapping of the native article.

The situation in the 1950s was therefore that engines of CR design were to be found in very many parts of Scotland, and that is a phenomenon which merits explanation, because it did not occur by chance. The first point to be made is that the engines must have been well designed, or the LMS would have scrapped them as soon as it could. A further proof of their quality is that although enginemen are, like most of us, conservative, and prefer the devil they know to the devil they don't, by and large CR engines were accepted by the men who had to run them in their new homes. Of course there must have been exceptions, but there doesn't seem to have been any of the wholesale rejection, and relegation to the back of the shed, which occurred on other railways when 'foreign' engines appeared after the Grouping. It seems to indicate them being good engines from everyone's point of view.

The next point to consider is why they kept on working when the rest had stopped, for the GSWR and the HR also had good engines. However, by comparison with the CR locomotives, they were few in number, and that must have told against them. It must also be true that the Caledonian Railway's enlightened policy of scrapping old engines and building new ones during the years of its prosperity, played a part in their survival. It may have reduced the

Plate 127: On the same day as the duty seen in *Plate 128*, another 'Pickersgill' was at work around Glasgow, at Bishopbriggs on the 1842 Edinburgh & Glasgow Railway main line, of all places. The train of three LNER coaches is the 4.37p.m. from Queen St. (High Level) to Perth, via Castlecary, the CR line over the swingbridge to Alloa (seen in *Plate 152*), the Devon Valley line to Kinross, and thence over Glenfarg Bank to Perth. This journey occupied 2½ hours, and going direct by the 'St Mungo' (5p.m. from Buchanan St.) took an hour less, but it would be worth the extra time just to visit Rumbling Bridge and Crook of Devon. No. 54485 was shedded at Perth, and certainly not polished like Carstairs' No. 54477. The colour-light signalling is controlled from Cowlairs, including the ground signal in the foreground for the crossover road, the points motor of which is beside the tender.

shareholders' dividends, but the result was that the average age of the locomotive stock at the Grouping was significantly less than that of most of the other Scottish railways. The GSWR was poorly off in this respect, and all but eleven of its engines were scrapped by 1939, and so were not saved by the wartime engine shortage.

Apart from the 4-4-0s, I don't think many enthusiasts would have described the surviving CR locomotives as outstandingly handsome. Happily, the changes made by the LMS were not ones which greatly detracted from their appearance, and even the stovepipe chimneys reminded the knowledgeable of the way things had been before Drummond arrived. They looked worst on

the 0-4-4 tanks, but almost proper on the 'Jumbos' which, by the 1950s, had a fairly archaic air to them anyway. The only other visual loss, besides chimney caps and the famous blue livery, was the smokebox wingplates on the 4-4-0s. The thing I regret, when I look at these pictures, is that so few of the old engines were clean, because if you compare *Plate 138* with *Plate 136*, you can see what a difference a shine makes to even the humblest locomotive. In the end, of course, the CR engines and equipment wore out and vanished from the scene, but these pictures may help to recall a little of their last, and not inglorious, years.

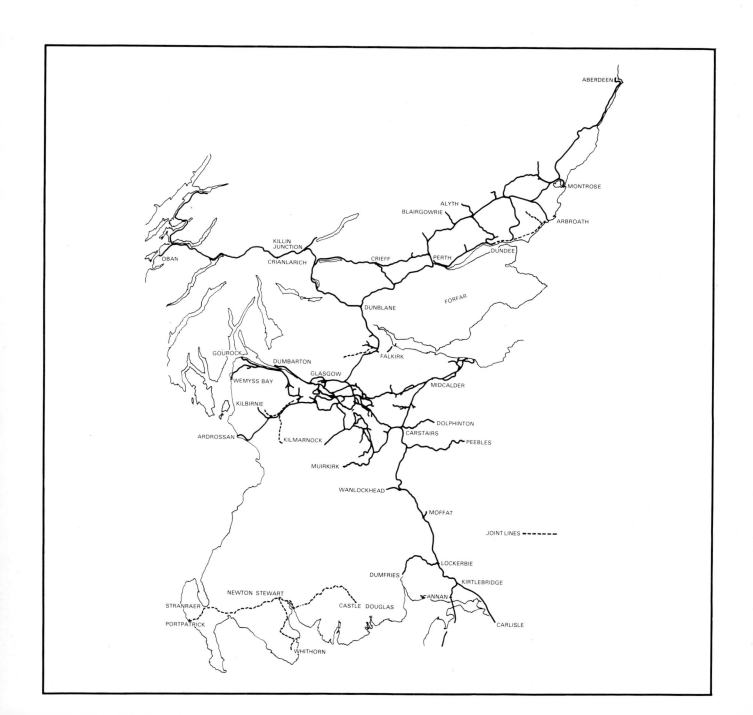

Plate 128: Envy the Lanarkshire commuters as they speed under clear signals through Uddingston on their way to Glasgow (Central) behind a 'Pickersgill'. No. 54477 was the first of the 1920 batch, and having it at the head of your train must have made going to work a pleasure. By 20th April 1957, when this picture of the 7.58a.m. from Lanark was taken, the coaches were BR, but who cared when you were streaking along the West Coast Main Line behind a polished 'Caley' 4-4-0.

Plate 129: McIntosh followed his successful express 4-4-0s with a similar design lengthened to produce an inside cylinder 4-6-0, of which *Cardean* was the best-known, but nevertheless most CR fast trains were worked by four-coupled engines, which William Pickersgill also built. However, in 1916, he also tried his hand at a 4-6-0 design, this time with outside cylinders, and produced the '60' class. The LMS multiplied them during 1925/6, the design being highly regarded by influential persons at St. Rollox, but thereafter the class had a very mixed reputation, especially on the GSWR section. They looked very impressive, but they were overshadowed by more modern LMS six-coupled types, although most of them lasted into BR ownership and some, like No. 54634, at Motherwell in 1951, were lined out as passenger engines. The object behind the chimney is the superheater relief or 'snifting' valve. These handsome 4-6-0s were all broken up by 1953.

Plate 130: One of the earliest railways in Scotland was the Dundee & Newtyle, and its original route northwards from Dundee climbed up two inclines worked by stationary steam engines. They were superseded in the 1860s by a line which ran along the north side of the Tay estuary, and then climbed on a long right-hand curve to reach the high ground north-west of the city. Its point of divergance from the line towards Perth was at Ninewells Junction, where we can see this deviation line, which was single, climbing alongside the Perth line. Latterly, the service from Dundee to Newtyle and beyond was very sparse, but this picture shows the tablet for the single line being taken at Ninewells Junction by the driver of No. 55169, working the 11.28a.m. train from Dundee (West), on 14 August 1954. The last passenger trains ran on 8th January 1955.

Plate 131: The Dundee & Newtyle Railway produced two diverging offspring, the Newtyle & Glamis to the east, and the Newtyle & Coupar Angus to the west. In time, parts of each of them became components of the main line from Perth to Aberdeen, with a 'cut-off' line joining their divergances, and avoiding a climb to Newtyle where through trains would have had to reverse. The 'cut-off' line ran from Ardler Junction on the Newtyle & Coupar Angus line to a point on the Newtyle & Glamis line which later became a double junction, by the building there of a branch northwards to Alyth, the station being named Alyth Junction. This picture shows the train from Dundee (West) standing in the 'down' main (Perth to Aberdeen) line platform there, after the CR 0-4-4 tank has run round, and is preparing to set off westwards towards Coupar Angus, the junction for its eventual destination of Blairgowrie. This manoeuvre was necessitated by the closure earlier in 1954 of the Newtyle to Ardler Juntion line. The branch to Alyth diverges to the left, behind the signal box, amid a forest of CR signals. The leading coach is a standard LMS compartment brake third of about 1927 vintage.

Plate 132: Blairgowrie had only one platform leading from its all-over roof, beneath which stands a single coach. The faithful No. 55169, having run round yet again, is propelling the two coaches it has brought from Dundee into the station, to couple up and form a three-coach train which will be worked back to Dundee (West) by the same route. Unfortunately few passengers took advantage of these complex manoeuvres, and like the Dundee & Newtyle Railway, the Blairgowrie branch lost its passenger service in January 1955, a far cry from that glorious day in 1907 when it actually accommodated a Royal Train. Looking at the front of No. 55169 one wonders what measures the crew took when they needed to open the smokebox door, for it has no handle of any sort, and someone has also made off with its shedplate. The nearer coach is again an LMS standard vehicle of their early pattern, built in the late 1920s.

Plate 133: The Caledonian Railway presence in Edinburgh was not extensive, and of their local services to Balerno, Barnton, and Leith, only the last was still operating in 1958. It was fitting that one of the 'passenger' batch of the '812' class, No. 57559 (old No. 821), should have been working the 1.43p.m. from Leith (North) to Princes Street on 24th April of that year, and especially so because this particular engine is thought to have been shedded at Edinburgh when new, and 60 years later was allocated to the CR shed, 64C being Edinburgh (Dalry Road). The leading coach is one of the LMS standard pattern brake thirds which became very common in Scotland with the withdrawal of pre-grouping vehicles before the war. The modest station at Leith with its little all-over roof, contrasting stongly with the splendours of Princes St., somehow reflects the relationship between the stone-built workaday atmosphere of Leith and the cosmopolitan elegance of Edinburgh next door. The method of supporting the left-hand side of the roof, using what look at a distance like old rails, is most unusual.

Plate 134: The last relic of the former CR local services in Edinburgh was the branch from Princes St. to Leith (North), worked by diesel trains from May 1958, just a month after this picture was taken, and closed to passengers in April 1962. The goods lines in the background relate to the numerous connections which this branch made with the docks on the south side of the Firth of Forth, while in the foreground, on the passenger lines, the 12.38p.m. from Leith to Princes St. has just shut off steam to stop at Newhaven. No. 55229 was one of the 1915 batch of 0-4-4 tanks built by Pickersgill, and in the last month of steam working was hauling a three-coach LMS-style corridor set painted red and cream, quite a glamorous ensemble for the Leith line. The centre coach is in fact a pre-war vehicle, but the others are of the 'porthole' type which BR built about 1950.

Plate 135: The standard Caledonian Railway 0-6-0 tanks were first built in 1898, and proved so useful that every few years of the company's existance, right down to 1922, a few more appeared. There were many parts of the system where an engine light on coal and water was ideal to undertake duties involving short-distance goods trips, some shunting, and periods of idleness, and this need was admirably met by McIntosh's '782' class. No. 56240 was at Aberdeen in 1954, waiting quietly for its services to be called upon, and was one of the diminishing band which had not lost its capped chimney, although the large dome is not original. It is also unusual in having no front numberplate, and the shed plate fixed high up on the smokebox door which is still airtight without the aid of a sealing ring and clips round the edge, additions which many former CR engines acquired in their last years.

Plate 136: At one time West Coast Anglo-Scottish expresses to Perth and the Highlands avoided Motherwell, and passed through Holytown on their way to Coatbridge and Larbert. It was also on the route of the CR Edinburgh to Glasgow service, whose trains from Princes St. to Central competed with those from Waverley to Queen St. The two-coach train, seen here in April 1957, did not enjoy such prestige, but rather was notable for its motive power. It is the 8.40a.m. from Hamilton, a service connecting into the 8.40a.m. Glasgow (Central) to Princes St. which is on the other side of the platform. Passengers making the connection for Edinburgh exchanged their '782' class CR 0-6-0 tank for an LMS 'Duchess'. However, No. 56296 did have some claim to fame, because it was one of the few members of its class fitted with the vacuum brake and steam heating. The use of this class on passenger work was decidedly unusual.

Plate 137: Motherwell Station, in 1959, presented a typical appearance for that part of the Scottish lowlands − smoke-blackened with lots of stone and hard-wearing pavement, and not a trace of any living greenery. To be fair, many Scottish stations in more prepossessing areas were decorated with flowering plants in hanging baskets. The train coming through the 'down' main platform was equally typical − mostly wagons for coal and steel, with the occasional container. The engine is No. 56367, one of the '782' class with its original dome, but a stovepipe chimney, and additionally what looks like a folded wagon sheet on top of the firebox. One must not complain − in France enginemen sometimes put a bicycle on the buffer beam.

Plate 139 (Right): Clydeside used to abound with works and shipyards, all rail-connected with lots of sharp curves on their sidings. Glasgow locomotive builders produced several varieties of 0-4-0 tank for industrial use, and so did the Caledonian Railway, with the difference that the 'main line' version often had to move over the running lines from one place to another during the day's work. As there might be no place to refuel, and the bunkers in the cab side sheets held only a small quantity, a coal-cart tender was often provided. No. 56031 is standing amid some typical Motherwell scenery in 1960, which contains colliery tips and a bogie bolster wagon loaded with girders for Argentina.

Plate 138 (Above): In 1911 McIntosh produced a six-wheeled close-coupled tank engine for the sharply curved dock sidings, and in the succeeding years 23 were built. They were, of course, much bigger and more powerful than the 0-4-0 tanks, one of which is just visible behind it in this picture at Ladyburn Shed, Greenock. Because of their compact and heavy appearance the '498' class were nicknamed 'Beetlecrushers'. Like all Caledonian tank engines from the 1880s onwards, they had the curved-topped design of side tanks, which Drummond had copied from Stroudley at Brighton. What is really unusual about this 1953 view is the cleanliness of the engine — with polished LMS date plate and the handrail reflecting in the front of the side tank, she was obviously somebody's favourite. These solid-looking machines lasted until 1962 when small diesels took over their duties.

Plate 140: This 1959 view of a 'Caley Pug' concentrates on the tender, if such a dignity can be given to that appendage. The scene is at Ibrox where the Govan and Princes Dock branches, connected with many industrial sidings, joined the Glasgow & Paisley Joint line. No. 56029 is setting off for home at the end of the day's work. The somewhat spartan accommodation for the enginemen is lit up by the evening sun, which also shows the large hole in the cab back sheet through which coal was shovelled on to the footplate. The fireman is standing on the tender, which appears to be of Caledonian Railway vintage. Someone has fixed a horseshoe over its drawhook, but the tail lamp is properly displayed for running here on the main line.

Plate 141: At Ibrox on the joint CR and GSWR line from Glasgow to Paisley there were two branches going northwards to the Clyde. One was to Govan, which closed to passengers in 1921. However its Ibrox platforms were still used in 1960 (to judge from the pale blue BR totem signs), perhaps by football trains terminating there in connection with the nearby Glasgow Rangers ground at Ibrox Park. No. 56260 is returning with a brake van after working on the other branch, to Princes Dock, in which the NBR had an interest. The signal guarding the exit from it is a typical CR example, on one of the lattice posts so common in Scotland.

Plate 142: Caledonian Railway engines were well built, worked hard, and had long lives. Many of them retained their original chimney caps, giving a certain dignity to an aged goods engine even if it was dirty. In 1955 this type was still to be found all over the old CR system, and at any of the multiple junctions in the industrial lowlands, such as Motherwell, one would see several in the space of an hour. This picture shows No. 57363 (old No. 560) built to a Drummond design by Lambie in 1892. The signal box is Lesmahagow Junction, showing the West Coast Main Line connection to Mossend, Coatbridge, and the north. The train headed by the 'Jumbo' is on a loop line.

Plate 143: Because it was part of the daily lot of the common goods engine to shunt on the often indifferent track in and around the private sidings of the collieries and works they served, the engines had to be fairly robust and not easily put out of order. A good example of both the situation and the locomotive is seen in this picture of a 'Jumbo', one of the 1887 products of St. Rollox Works. It is seen in April 1962 near Shieldmuir Junction in Lanarkshire, with a short train. The problem of keeping the smokebox door airtight on an engine 75 years old has called for the application of a battery of clips round its edge, but nevertheless there are signs that the freshly painted door was not truly sealed, and has been burned yet again. As CR engines did not originally have lamp irons on the front buffer beam, the 'piano front' has a hole cut into it below the smokebox door, to accommodate the centre lamp iron when it is opened towards us. This is No. 52799.

Plate 144: When Drummond's basic goods 0-6-0s first appeared in 1883 they were nicknamed 'Jumbos', and no doubt blessed by a locomotive running department at its wits end for up-to-date engines. The first of the St. Rollox batch to be put to work, in November 1883, was No. 349, and this picture of it as BR No. 57237 was taken almost 80 years later, on the CR main line north of Shieldmuir Junction, where the connection from Wishaw (Central) trails in. Altogether, 244 of this type were built by Drummond and his successors. In LMS and BR days many had stovepipe chimneys, new domes, and pop valves, while the tender of No. 57237 is also not the original. The long train is operating under a 'Local Instruction', for although it is on the main line, it has a guard's brake only at the front. Let us hope that the last vehicle at least carried a tail lamp.

Plate 145: The 4-4-0s built from 1916 to 1922 were based on the 'Dunalastair IV' class, but always known as 'Pickersgills' after their designer, and could be distinguished from the McIntosh variety by their straight coupling rod splashers. No. 54483 in unlined black livery, with BRITISH RAILWAYS on the tender, is running into Buchanan St. Station, in Glasgow, early one morning in August 1953, with a rather mixed collection of coaches, the first of which is a flush-panelled LNER vehicle, followed by an LMS twelve-wheeled 1936 dining car. The lower quadrant shunting signal underhung from the gantry on the right is CR, and just below it, on a gantry in the distance beyond the bridge, the station lampman is about his morning's work.

Plate 146: One of the famous 'Grampian Corridor' type of 68ft. long twelve-wheelers, first built in 1905 for use on the best services between Glasgow and Aberdeen, and subsequently, with modifications, for other services where there was intense competition. Their size and splendour gave the management of the rival NBR a terrible inferiority complex, and for some years they were the finest coaches in Scotland. English trains could produce little or nothing to rival them. Despite the peeling paint, and total insensitivity in the matter of relating the livery to the waist panelling, this coach still has a characteristic of the Caledonian Railway — it has style.

Plate 147: When the Caledonian Railway pushed northwards over the Clyde to a new Central Station in Glasgow, in 1879, the Clyde Trustees limited them to a four track bridge across the river, which this train from England is traversing. Another bridge with nine tracks was built downstream, on the left, in conjunction with the rebuilding of Central Station in the early years of this century and, in 1908, a completely new electro-pneumatic signalling installation was completed. This 1960 picture shows, on the left between the two bridges, the 1908 signal box and, interspersed between the overhead girders of the old bridge, some of the signals of the same period. They were novel in having numbered route indictors to show which platform the train was signalled into (this train is heading for platform 1), instead of a separate signal for each route, which was the normal practice in those days. In the far distance there is an 0-4-4 tank on station pilot duty. This old bridge was closed at the beginning of 1961.

Plate 148: Although once commonly seen on passenger duties, by March 1959 the '812' class were rarely employed on such trains as the 12.28p.m. Rutherglen to Balloch. On its way to the 'Dead and Buried' (Dumbarton & Balloch Joint line) it will have traversed Glasgow (Central) Low Level and contributed to the smoky gloom of a station where, on a wet day, passengers almost had to feel their way to the trains. At one time CR engines used on the Glasgow Central Railway (to give the Low Level lines their proper title) had condensers, but in BR days such things were long past. In this view, the train has left the depths of the Low Level, and is climbing in the daylight as it approaches Partick East Junction where the line to Maryhill, via Crow Road and Kelvinside, goes off to the north. The engine is No. 57607, with the Dubs & Co. 1900 works plate just visible on the centre splasher, and the coaches are LMS, with a brake third of the 1930s leading some older stock. Note the Stevens & Co. 'drop-down' ground signal, so common on Scottish lines, which is in the centre foreground.

Plate 149: This goods train at Flemington includes two of the new BR four-wheeled flush-sided vans with end doors (covered carriage trucks to the older generation of railwaymen), as well as a similar vehicle of a much earlier design, and a passenger coach underframe converted to carry cars in the open. They are being propelled southwards along one of the independent lines beside the West Coast Main Line, the motive power for this movement being '782' class No. 56307, one of the many with a stovepipe chimney.

Plate 150: Terminus Junction is a point just south of the Clyde in Glasgow where the CR routes from the east connect with the lines to Paisley, and with various goods stations like the recently closed riverside General Terminus. The line here was opened as part of the Pollok & Govan Railway in the 1840s, and in this 1960 view was still a place where plenty of steam-hauled goods trains could be seen. Today not only is steam haulage a thing of the past, but so is the loose-coupled goods train. The stock in this one is typical of the 1950s, a mixture of pre and post-nationalisation vehicles, with a Southern Railway box van leading, a GWR ventilated van next, and then a general assortment, some with leaky roofs that have been covered with wagon sheets for the journey. The engine is one of the first batch of the '812' class, No. 57555, built in 1899, and originally painted passenger blue for working the very competitive services between Glasgow and the Clyde Coast, among others. For this work the engines were fitted with the Westinghouse brake, but vacuum brake equipment was substituted in LMS days, and the pipes associated with it have been rather crudely run along the footplate valance of the engine and tender.

Plate 151: Beside the rock-bound coast, the Banff branch train pulls away from the terminus in August 1954. This is a 'three company' train, with CR 0-4-4 tank No. 55185 followed by a Great North of Scotland carriage, painted red and cream, no doubt by gross favouritism at Inverurie Works where it was built and maintained. Behind, there is a North British bogie which had not been so favoured. This little line closed in 1964, perhaps managing to hold out so long by acquiring traffic from the other GNSR line to Banff, which closed in 1961.

Plate 152: The unruffled waters of the Forth provide a perfect mirror image of the single line swing bridge at Alloa which the CR opened in 1885. The train is on the first of the spans, with the 150ft. opening span surmounted by its octagonal engine house, in the distance. The NBR used this route for goods trains until their second Tay Bridge was opened in 1887. Alloa swing bridge was demolished in 1971 and like the first Tay Bridge, only wave-washed piers remain to tell of its glory.

Plate 153: Another duty latterly in the hands of a CR 0-4-4 tank was the quiet NBR branch from Balmano Junction at Bridge of Earn, to Newburgh and Ladybank. The trains started from Perth, and even in NBR days were worked by veteran locomotives. Despite operating in such a backwater, or perhaps because he only saw four trains a day, the porter at Abernethy kept his station in good trim with an abundance of flowers, even on the site of the track removed in 1933. The local passenger trains were withdrawn in 1955, a year after the 4p.m. from Perth to Ladybank called but, in 1975, the Perth to Edinburgh services started using this route, which remains in use. In the foreground is one of the very narrow and quite distinctive NBR three-wheeled platform trolleys. The engine's shed plate is unusually above the numberplate, and the chimney, by comparison with the one seen in *Plate 151*, appears suspiciously like the NBR variety.

Plate 154: The little station at Killin must have held some sort of a record for the brevity of its awning over the platform, and seems little changed since 1886 when the steep line down at 1 in 70 from Killin Junction on the Callander & Oban line was opened. Behind the train the track goes on to the remote pier on Lock Tay, but for many years passenger trains had gone no further than Killin. As the clouds over Ben Lawers signify, this picture of CR 0-4-4 tank No. 55195 was taken in a brief sunny interval between Highland rain storms. A few minutes later, amid a downpour of rain, the one coach train set off back to Killin Junction, where it connected with the service from Oban to Glasgow (Buchanan St.). In March 1959, this short branch was one of the dwindlig band of places where the CR 0-4-4 tanks were still active, but it closed in 1965.

Anybody who writes about the Glasgow & South Western section does so in the shadow of that wonderful raconteur, the late and much-missed David L. Smith. His magic was that he didn't write about railways, engines, and men, but about the men and their work. The equipment was an essential part of the story he had to tell, but it was woven round the people, whose acquaintance he enjoyed for a lifetime. I begin, then, with a rare piece of guaranteed good advice. If you have not done so yet, read his books on the GSWR section, and you will realise why I hesitate in beginning this very brief account.

St. Enoch Station in Glasgow is where I first made the acquaintance of the Glasgow & South Western section. Like its cousin, St. Pancras in London, it was a station elevated above the surrounding streets, presumably to be on a level with the bridge over the Clyde a few chains from the end of the platform. In consequence passengers approached it by a ramp up from St. Enoch Square, which once showed me a memorable Glasgow sight. Taxis stood by the station entrance at the top of the ramp and, as the leading one set off with a passenger, I saw the white-bearded driver of the next cab climb out and push it to the head of the rank, rather than start the engine. Only in Glasgow... or perhaps in Aberdeen. Again, like St. Pancras, a hotel crowned the station entrance, although a more restrained – and dare I say Scottish – building, compared with Scott's neo-Gothic performance in London. From the 1890s it faced the breezy baroque confection of 'the other St. Enoch', the principal station on Glasgow's Subway, which occupies the centre of the square. St. Enoch's Church, disgusted at the pair of them, departed in 1925.

Inside, the station had a most impressive train shed. Its two arches, one large and one small, were each formed in a continuous curve even more satisfying than St. Pancras' slightly pointed arch, and the radial pattern of the outer end glazing enhanced the effect. *(Plate 156)*. In the early BR years, it was also very pleasing to a photographer in search of pre-grouping designs, because a substantial part of its train services was worked by 4-4-0s, although this happy state of affairs had a sad origin. The GSWR engine stock had been in a poor way in 1923, and despite some ingenious head scratching in St. Rollox drawing office, no way could be found to get the new Northern Division standard boilers (ex-Caledonian) into GSWR engines. Given the supposed hostility between the two companies before the Grouping, it might seem surprising that they even tried, but perhaps the 'Caley' felt they could be magnanimous now that they were the senior part of the LMS in Scotland. This failure to find a way to renew the GSWR engines caused four-fifths of them to be scrapped by 1933. Their replacements were, until the mid-1930s, either Caledonian engines or LMS-built Midland types. So in the early 1950s, St. Enoch provided Caledonian 'Dunalastairs' and 'Pickersgills', with Midland Compounds and 2Ps for variety. The station pilots were CR 0-4-4 tanks. What more could a photographer ask for?

Once out of St. Enoch and across the Clyde the GSWR divided. Trains going west to Renfrew on the Clyde, round to Ayr and beyond, went via Paisley, while trains for the south made for Kilmarnock, via Barrhead, climbing Neilston Bank to the summit at the Shilford, 11½ miles out on a line that had once been joint with the Caledonian. There are many tales told of sprints northbound down this bank towards Glasgow, but my remembrance of it is battling through Neilston, southbound on the sleeper to St. Pancras, our overloaded engine going slower and slower on the last stage of the climb as if knowing of the bets that were being made by the boys in the train, about whether we would turn the top or not. The doubters lost, but only just. One slip would have done it. David Smith tells the story of one of the then new Class 2P 4-4-0s sent forth from St. Enoch, bound for the south, with a Class 4P Compound's load. Well it looked the same as a

Compound, and I expect it was making the same heavy weather of its load over the last mile to the summit as we were with the sleeper. By the 1950s, the Compounds were on their way out as far as the GSWR was concerned, but the Class 2Ps kept Derby's flag flying. By then they didn't normally work the hardest jobs, but some of them at least were still well looked after, if external appearance is anything to go by, perhaps by men who remembered their glorious youth *(Plate 165)*.

The majority of services leaving St. Enoch did not have to try conclusions with the Shilford, but ran via Paisley with a choice of two parallel routes. Like the Barrhead road the northern of these was joint with the Caledonian at one time, while the southern line belonged to the GSWR alone. This was the very curvacious 'Canal Road' through Paisley (Canal) Station to join the other route at Elderslie. The 'Joint' line, however, also carried the trains from Glasgow (Central) serving Wemyss Bay, Gourock, and Greenock (Central). It certainly needed four tracks to accommodate its traffic. With several good places for photography and lots of suburban trains, it surprises me that so few pictures taken on it have been published. But that is true of the whole GSWR section. The 'Caley' had the glamorous expresses and the Highland had the scenery, but the Sou' West had David Smith. I spent many happy hours on the Joint line as you can see, and it was well worth doing. Trains for the Caledonian route to Greenock, etc. could use only the Joint line, but the connections at Glasgow and Paisley were such that GSWR trains could use the Joint or the Canal road. The choice was, I think, a matter of pathways and line occupation, although in the heroic days of the fast expresses the Joint line was preferred because it was straighter. Incidentally the 'Canal road' got its name from the fact that it was built, in 1885, on the site of the Paisley & Johnstone Canal, which was no doubt the source of all those curves.

The GSWR line to Greenock (Princes Pier) was closed beyond Kilmacolm in 1959, and completely in 1983, so all trains now use the CR route beyond Paisley. The 'Canal road' was also closed in 1983. At one time there was keen competition between CR and GSWR for the passenger traffic of places like Dunoon and Brodick. The GSWR route to Princes Pier involved a severe climb in either direction to Upper Port Glasgow (Goods), but the 'Caley' had an easier road close to river level for much of the distance. In the 1950s, of course, these routes were no longer in active competition. The GSWR engines were long-since gone, and its Clyde Coast trains could be seen leaving St. Enoch behind Caledonian as well as Midland/LMS engines. It was not uncommon in high summer, when Corkerhill and Greenock sheds were stretched to the limit in the demand for engines, for 0-6-0s to be used. The coming of LMS-type 2-6-4 tanks heralded the beginning of the end for 4-4-0 haulage. Then the electrics came, but I like to look at the picture of old No. 595 storming down the Joint line on the way to Ayr with express lamps up *(Plate 180)*, and dream of the 5.10 p.m. non-stop which she used to work.

The carriages behind these engines seemed to be almost exclusively LMS, many of the early Midland-derived period with full panelling. By the early 1960s even they were being displaced by BR stock. Pre-grouping carriages were very rare, although the odd Caledonian put in an appearance, but I could find no GSWR coaching stock at all. There was, however, a certain amount of signalling equipment about which dated from before 1923. Where lower quadrants were still in use they greatly resembled those on the other Scottish railways, particularly in their fondness for steel lattice posts. One minor but observable difference from the Caledonian was in the GSWR spectacle plates which were a curious hybrid shape. The 'off' or green spectacle was the common elongated oval which gave a positive colour indication when the arm was lowered, whether to 30 degrees from the horizontal or more sharply, if heat had caused the wire to expand. The 'on' or red spectacle however was not a similar shape (as for example on the Caledonian) but round. Subsidiary signals seemed to have two round spectacles, widely separated and reminding me of Midland style. Signalling on the Glasgow and Paisley Joint line was, I think, Caledonian. One other sign of the 'Caley take-over' was that the LMS and BR decreed the carrying of CR-type route indicating semaphores on the engines of GSWR passenger trains using St. Enoch. By the 1950s this rule was observed somewhat patchily, although Greenock drivers were careful to abide by it.

More of the Sou' West has been lost to us, in proportion, than of the other Scottish constituents of the LMS. The main line to Carlisle through Kilmarnock and Dumfries remains open, as does that mountainous route south to Stranraer. Most of the Ayrshire lines, admittedly built more for minerals than passengers, have been closed, and the 'Caley' might be though to have won the last battle for Greenock. Even great St. Enoch, the first public building in Scotland to be lit by electricity, was closed to passengers in 1966, although steam could be seen there almost to the end. The Caledonian's Buchanan Street terminus closed the same year, so perhaps honours are even on that score at least. But despite all that has been lost, the Glasgow & South Western Railway will never be forgotten because of the undying work of David L. Smith.

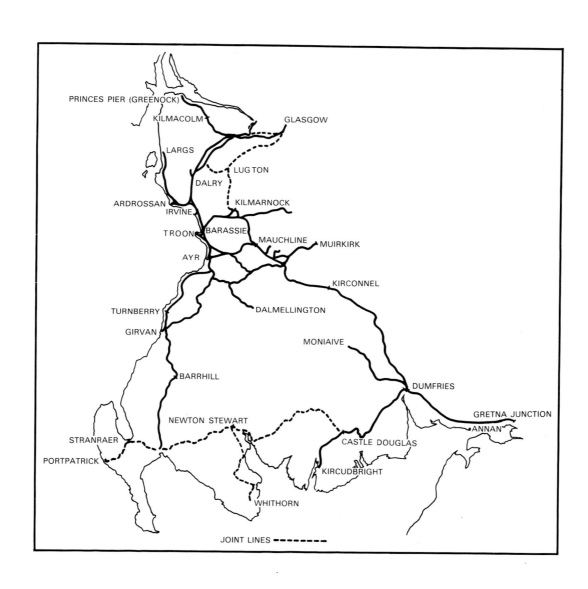

JOINT LINES ━ ━ ━ ━ ━ ━

Plate 155: Caledonian Railway locomotive No. 139 was the first to the 'Dunalastair IV' class to be built with a superheater, indeed the first Scottish engine so fitted, when it left St. Rollox works in 1910. As BR No. 54440, it was on the GSWR section 42 years later, leaving St. Enoch with a train to Greenock. The paint may be peeling off the leading coach, which is LMS, but somebody at Greenock (Ladyburn) Shed cared enough for the engine to see that it was cleaned — an old 'Caley' man perhaps? Note the CR hooter prominent above the cab roof and the Pickersgill one-piece chimney.

Plate 156: Passengers for Campbeltown, on the Mull of Kintyre, could leave Glasgow (Central) just after 8a.m. and take a ship at Gourock, or save 1½ hours and catch the 9.50a.m. from St. Enoch to Fairlie Pier. If they preferred a lie in bed they would have found Compound No. 40909 at the head of the Campbeltown Boat Train on 26th September 1955. The station's notable roofline is in the background, and so is the night sleeper from St. Pancras.

W.A.C. Smith

Plate 157: This picture of Class 2P No. 40624 illustrates one of St. Enoch's advantages — the long platform on the sunny side, just right for photographing departing local trains. This one is bound for Ardrossan, in August 1953, and is formed of carriages which are typical of those used on short-distance GSWR section trains at that date. They are of LMS build, derived from Midland Railway practice, the first two being complete with elaborate external mouldings which were part of the finish given to all passenger stock until about 1929.

Plate 158: Caledonian Railway engines were built with only one lamp iron, at the base of the chimney. The LMS gave them another three in the usual places on the buffer beam, and often also fitted edge dogs round the smokebox door when it began to warp, and handles in place of the original wheel which '812' class 0-6-0 No. 57594 retains. Built by Sharp, Stewart & Co. at their Atlas works Glasgow in 1900, by 1953 it was still in the city, but working on the GSWR section, detaching some vans from the tail of a train which had arrived at St. Enoch.

Plate 159: Before leaving St. Enoch we ought to notice the humble carriage pilot, one of the early Caledonian 0-4-4 tanks built with condensing gear for the Central Station Low Level lines. The plain black livery with block characters was widely applied to ex-LMS engines in Scotland in the early days of nationalisation, presumably by St. Rollox Works.

Plate 160: 'Starlight Specials' were an early attempt by British Railways to offer a cut-price no-frills overnight service between England and Scotland. If the bar wasn't open all night it certainly stayed open very late, although never long enough for some customers. As the July evening shadows lengthen, Class 2P No. 40573 pilots 5XP 'Jubilee' No. 45573 *Newfoundland* getting its heavy train well on the move for the climb to the Shilford. The train is passing Strathbungo, the second station on the Glasgow, Barrhead & Kilmarnock Joint line.

W.A.C. Smith

Plate 161: The GB&K Joint line station at Pollockshaws was given the suffix (West) to distinguish it from the 'Caley' establishment on the Cathcart Circle line. The fine platform lamps are only one of the details worth study as the faithfully Class 2P calls with a Joint line 'stopper' in May 1961.

W.A.C. Smith

Plate 162: The 5.18p.m. Kilmarnock to St. Enoch train accellerates past empty sidings between Pollockshaws (West) and Crossmyloof, on the final stage of its run down from the Shilford into Glasgow. The engine caught by the autumn sunshine is LMS Class 2P No. 40642 but, in September 1960, BR carriages are beginning to appear.

W.A.C. Smith

Plate 163: No. 40913 was Corkerhill shed's first Compound when it arrived in 1927. By 1954, when this picture was taken at Neilston on the GB&K Joint line, it had enjoyed a spell of Highland air *(see Plate 205)* and, on return, was caught working the 1.40p.m. Glasgow (South Side) to Dumfries milk empties, one LNER four-wheeler. Is the bent smokebox door handrail evidence of some disagreement north of Perth?

Plate 164: Exactly a year after the view in *Plate 158* was photographed, No. 57594 is in action again, rather more strenuously in the GB&K Joint line this time. It is blasting its way up the last few yards to the summit at the Shilford with a Class D partially-fitted goods train and, in view of the heavy work involved, it is as well that the bottom of the smokebox door has been fitted with some extra securing dogs. The fastening wheel has been replaced by a handle. It says something for Sharp, Stewart's workmanship that the engine was still up to this sort of task after 55 years.

Plate 165: With paintwork gleaming from the efforts of the cleaners at Hurlford Shed, Kilmarnock, Class 2P No. 40618 storms out of Neilston, southbound, attacking the last mile up to the summit at the Shilford with the 7.39pm. St. Enoch to Kilmarnock train on 8th August 1953. On a lattice post to the right of the engine are two of Stevens & Co.'s 'drop-down' shunting signals, which were to be found at one time on most of Scotland's railways, except the Highland.

Plate 166: Caldwell Station on the GB&K Joint line was only about 1½ miles south of the Shilford Summit, and therefore a welcome sight for the crews of northbound trains, so long as they were still going strong, that is. Class 2P No. 40612 was booked to call there, so they had no worries on this trip. This line's joint ownership was the result of a general shortage of capital for railways in the late 1860s, because in that troubled decade neither the CR or the GSWR could afford the cost of an independent direct line from Glasgow to Kilmarnock.

Plate 167: With Caldwell Station in the distance, Class 2P No. 40686 sets off down the hill to Kilmarnock with the 7.10p.m. from St. Enoch, on 7th August 1954. The shapely Midland style chimney is prominent (see *Plate 166* for the Stanier variety), and the buffer beam has been well cleaned so that all can see which shed was responsible for the polish on the engine, although not the tender. Oddly enough most of the engines of this class on the Midland section lost their original chimneys quite early in their lives.

Plate 168: A cloud of escaping steam from Compound No. 41127 hides the engine shed at Stranraer as this train sets out on its long journey through Galloway, over the Portpatrick & Wigtownshire Joint Line to Castle Douglas and Dumfries. The nearest the GSWR got to Stranraer was Challoch Junction, seven miles out. Today, the 'PP&W' is closed completely except for this seven miles, by which trains from England as well as Glasgow now reach Stranraer.

A.E. Bennett

Plate 169: The enginemen walking down the platform would seem to indicate that Compound No. 41131 has been re-manned at Castle Douglas before continuing to Dumfries and Carlisle. There are two fish vans at the head of the train, indicating Stranraer as the likely starting point. There are no trains at Castle Douglas today, but in 1955 you could still change there for Kirkudbright.

W.A.C. Smith

Plate 170: GSWR rolling stock was very hard to find in the 1950s, but some survived as departmental vehicles. This six-wheeled passenger brake by James Manson dates from the early 1890s, and was being used as a tool van in 1959. (BR No. M297267).

W.A.C. Smith

Plate 171: Like father and son these two members of the Caledonian 'Jumbo' family pose in the sunshine outside their home shed at Dumfries on the GSWR. No. 57302 is a true 'Jumbo' and cost £1,700 in 1887, while No. 57623 was an 1899 member of McIntosh's '812' class, costing £2,190. Although, by 1959, they might claim to have done their share of work for their various owners, they were still active, and looked after, as their condition shows.

W.A.C. Smith

Plate 172: The last train to call at Bellahouston was the 5.46p.m. from St. Enoch to Paisley (West), on 18th September 1954. There were no speeches, or crowds on the platform to wave goodbye as CR 0-4-4 tank No. 55211 pulls away, only the photographer to record the event for us. Did the guard, as he looked back from his brake, realise he had just made a little bit of railway history?

W.A.C. Smith

Plate 173: Like most van trains, this St. Enoch to Ayr special is a scratch collection of vehicles, the sequence from the tender being four-wheeled, bogie, and six-wheeled. Has Ayr's Class 2P, No. 40574, had a new smokebox? We can see that the Midland chimney has been replaced, by comparison with others of the class in this chapter. Behind the engine is what could be mistaken for an elevated greenhouse, but is, in fact, Bellahouston signal box.

W.A.C. Smith

Plate 174: Not another 'Jumbo' but a Highland Railway class that ended its days far from home, the 'Barneys' were the work of Dugald Drummond's younger brother, Peter, before he came to the GSWR in 1912. Their ancestry is obvious, although for some reason the LMS classed them '3F' while a 'Jumbo' was only '2F'. In the early days of BR, No. 17698 is still in LMS Livery trundling tender-first along the Glasgow & Paisley Joint line, near Hillington West. It has a CR boiler as well as the diamond-shaped Dubs & Co. works plate on the centre splasher.

J.L. Stevenson

Plate 175: Caledonian engines were used by the LMS to replace GSWR shunting tanks as they wore out. This trio is at Corkerhill Shed, opened in the 1890s to replace the old and overcrowded shed at St. Enoch. The first and third of these engines are members of the '782' or 'Standing Shunting' class but the middle one is an outside-cylinder 'Beetlecrusher' 0-6-0 tank, used for sharp curves in dock sidings. Behind them is Corkerhill village, built for its staff by the GSWR when Corkerhill was quite out in the country, so there are half-timbered gables in the best Norman Shaw style. (The locomotive on the left is No. 56364).

W.A.C. Smith

Plate 176: Another 'Barney' on the GSWR section, No. 57695 stands rather forlornly outside the village at Corkerhill June 1949, having been renumbered a year previously. At least it kept its chimney cap when a Caledonian type boiler was fitted, and it survived until withdrawal in January 1952 — the last 'Barney' at work.

H.C. Casserley

Plate 177: This picturesque view with spring buds on the trees and a stream flowing quietly by, might mislead one to think that the 2p.m. from Largs to St. Enoch sweeping round the corner behind Class 2P No. 40624 is out in the Ayrshire countryside, but it is in fact in the vicinity of Corkerhill, on the Canal line, less than five miles from the centre of Glasgow.

W.A.C. Smith

Plate 178: Mosspark (West), opened by the LMS to serve a new housing estate, got its suffix because most of the new Mosspark suburb was immediately north of Corkerhill Station. In 1954 a new station building is under construction as a stopping train from the Ayrshire coast calls to pick up some local residents who are going into Glasgow for the afternoon. With a ten-coach load and a 6ft. 9in. 4-4-0, it cannot have been an easy job stopping and starting at every station, although GSWR section crews were very attached to their long-serving Class 2Ps.

W.A.C. Smith

Plate 179: Local services on the Canal line ran between St. Enoch and Paisley (West) over a very curving route, so it is appropriate that the 5.13p.m. train from Glasgow, seen here leaving Paisley (Canal) Station, is on a sharp curve. As usual, the engine is a Class 2P 4-4-0, No. 40620. The signal box with its deep eaves, large paned windows, and a gas lamp on the front, is typical of GSWR practice when the Canal line opened in 1885.

W.A.C. Smith

Plate 180: Ayr's No. 40595 was once a famous racer down the Joint line to Paisley and Ayr and here, thirty years later but still with express lights up, she comes romping through Ibrox with an evening commuter train from St. Enoch. Alas, the condition of the smokebox door reminds us that quite a few miles have rolled by since 1928, but the shine on the tender also tells a tale. The signals above and below the footbridge are of the Caledonian Railway pattern.

Plate 181: A Caledonian 0-6-0 casts a pall of smoke over Ibrox and district as it heads west towards Paisley with a heavy train. The lines going off to the left lead to Govan and Princes Dock *(see Plate 141)*. There are several open wagons at the front of this train which are sheeted over a tilt (a raised bar running the length of the wagon's centre), and by the early 1960s that was something of a rarity.

Plate 182: The east end of the layout at Ibrox on a fine evening with the 'commuter rush' in full swing. Exceptionally, the Class 2P is dirty, and the paint is peeeling off. The 5.25p.m. St. Enoch to Ardrossan train was the only 'business train' to stop here, although the buses along the main road had taken most of its traffic from town. The branch on the left only saw passenger trains when football specials were run for matches at the nearby Glagow Rangers stadium, and the cast-iron rustic seat on the right, although a nice touch against the grass of the cutting, saw equally few customers.

Plate 183: The GSWR reached the Clyde at Renfrew Wharf, but latterly the branch from Arkleston Junction in Paisley carried passenger trains only in the morning and evening 'peaks'. This is the 5.36p.m. from Renfrew, calling at Paisley (Abercorn), on 31st July 1958. The line has been singled and only the 'down' platform is in use. As Class 2P No. 40636 brakes to a halt, the ticket collector stands waiting, and the carriage doors swing open to let these two mile commuters jump from the train.

W.A.C. Smith

Plate 184: Gilmour Street was and remains Paisley's principal station, in 1955 still with its awnings supported by lattice girders, so keeping the platforms themselves unimpeded by the normal awning stanchions. The Glasgow & Paisley Joint line ended here. By 1955 Caledonian 4-4-0s were working the GSWR section trains to Greenock (Princes Pier) as well as their own to Gourock, and No. 54468 is at the head of the 12.17p.m. train from Princes Pier to St. Enoch.

W.A.C. Smith

Plate 185: British Railways retained both the GSWR and Caledonian piers at Ardrossan, the latter (Montgomerie Pier) serving the steamers running to the Isle of Man and Belfast. In 1955 the 8.05p.m. Belfast Boat Train from Montgomerie Pier was allowed only 50 minutes for the 33 miles to Glasgow (Central), with a single stop at Paisley, so Compound No. 40913 was still going hard at Elderslie, two miles from Gilmour Street. Elderslie Station had the junction of the Joint and the Canal lines on one side, and that between the Greenock and the Ayr lines on the other. The station closed in 1966.

W.A.C. Smith

Plate 186: Ten years after the picture at St. Enoch was taken CR 4-4-0 No. 54440 was in even better condition. It has lost its front numberplate but the left-hand footplating has been straightened out *(see Plate 155)*. The train amid the gaslamps and greenery of Kilmacolm is the 2.04p.m. from St. Enoch to Greenock (Princess Pier), carrying, as most trains on this line seemed to, the 'ten to eight' setting of the semaphore route indicator.

W.A.C. Smith

Plate 187: No. 57566, one of McIntosh's standard goods, or '812' class, on a Clyde Coast service, the 3.05p.m. from St. Enoch to Princes Pier. This engine's first duties in 1899 were on the rival CR route to Gourock which kept to lower ground closer to the river away to the left, leaving the windy heights of Upper Port Glasgow (Goods) to the GSWR. No. 57566 is still with us, preserved and on loan to the Strathspey Railway.

W.A.C. Smith

Plate 188: High above Port Glasgow a Caledonian 'Dunalastair IV' crosses the Devol Viaduct on its way to St. Enoch with a train from Greenock. No. 54453 is still in the early unlined black BR livery in 1954, but the cleaners have raised a shine on the boiler, which is a good sign. Compared with the CR route which passes close to the shore-side gasholder, the difficulties facing GSWR crews are obvious.

W.A.C. Smith

Plate 189: Lynedoch was the last station before Princes Pier and closed in 1959. Clean, but leaking a little steam, No. 54441 has stopped briefly with an afternoon service from St. Enoch. Despite or perhaps because of the industrial surroundings, the station staff were keen gardeners, and passengers in the summer of 1954 were treated to flowers in beds, in tubs, and in hanging baskets, as well as 'Dunalastair IVs' on trains.

W.A.C. Smith

Plate 190: It took a long time for conditions on the railways to improve after the desperate shortages of wartime. This may account for the poor condition of Compound No. 41148 at Princes Pier in 1951. Like Paisley (Gilmour Street), this station's awnings were supported on cross girders rather than stanchions. It opened in 1894 and saw its last passengers in 1966.

W.A.C. Smith

Plate 191: A strong Caledonian presence at Greenock (Princes Pier) was manifest in July 1955 in the shape of a 'Pickersgill', No. 54492, newly out of shops and needing a clean, and the leading carriage which is a late vintage CR semi-corridor third brake. Like the '60' class 4-6-0s, the 'Pickersgills' had a superheater relief valve behind the chimney.

W.A.C. Smith

Plate 192: Pulling out of Greenock (Princes Pier) by the site of the previous Albert Harbour Station, 'Pickersgill' No. 54506, with a St. Enoch train, passes under a fine gantry of distinctive GSWR signals. The engine is one of the last CR 4-4-0s built, in 1922, and retains its original and very shapely dome, while the carriages are mostly LMS of the late 1920s. I suppose the people living in the houses on the right were resigned to firemen who smoked them out as they prepared for the stiff climb to Upper Port Glasgow.

I think you can divide the old Highland Railway into three parts. First, and first in point of time, there is what might be called the 'low Highland', which is the lines along the south coast of the Moray Firth from Inverness to Nairn, Forres, Elgin, and Keith Junction. There were branches to the coast at Hopeman and Fort George. I would also include the line through Beauly to Dingwall, and the long branch into the Black Isle, ending at Fortrose. All these lines between the mountains and the sea were without any prolonged heavy gradients. The branches mostly lost their passenger services in 1931 but remained open for goods well into the 1950s, or even later.

Totally different in character is the second part of the Highland system which Americans would probably call the 'Mountain Division'. It comprises the Perth to Inverness line from Stanley Junction on the now-closed CR Perth to Aberdeen route, over Druimuachdar Summit to Aviemore. The original line to Inverness then climbed over another summit, at Dava, before descending to Forres on the coastal line. A cut-off was opened in 1898 to run more directly to Inverness, over yet another summit, at Slochd. Banking or piloting assistance was provided on all three of these long gradients. It was performed by old HR 4-4-0s until the late 1940s when they wore out, and thereafter by 'Pickersgills' drafted in from the Caledonian, which lasted pretty well to the end of steam haulage in the Highlands. The original northern end of the main line, from Aviemore, over Dava, to Forres, closed in 1965.

The third part of the old Highland system comprises the 63 miles of the one-time Dingwall & Skye Railway, and the Far North line from Dingwall to Wick and Thurso. There was also at one time the Wick & Lybster Light Railway, closed in 1944, and branches to Strathpeffer and Dornoch. Although these routes have plenty of the ups and downs to be expected in mountainous country, there are none of the long banks, mile after mile at 1 in 70, which lie between Perth and Inverness. As, in general, the loads of trains north of Inverness were much less than south of it, there was not nearly so much piloting to be done there in steam days.

The Highland Railway engines which BR inherited were a mixed bunch, as to age, type, and usefulness. Of passenger engines there were both 4-4-0 and 4-6-0 classes, the former dating back to 1896 and being mostly Peter Drummond's 'Small Ben' class with inside cylinders (Plate 227). These had a strong family resemblance to the LSWR T9 class as built, and to Dugald Drummond's 4-4-0s on the NBR and the Caledonian, the latter passing on their general appearance to the early CR 'Dunalastairs'. The 4-6-0s looked much more modern. Built in 1918/19 they had outside cylinders with Walschaert's valve gear. In theory there were passenger and goods varieties, but both sorts could be seen on passenger trains. The Class 4P engines ('Clan' class) were extinct by 1950 but the so-called 'Clan Goods' (Class 4F), which closely resembled them, continued to do a great deal of passenger work for another year or two, especially on the Dingwall & Skye line. There were also the Drummond goods 0-6-0s, the 'Barneys', which ended their days at Corkerhill, the GSWR Glasgow shed. Lastly, and definitely in a class by themselves, working the eight-mile branch from The Mount to Dornoch, were the very last Highland engines to remain in service, a pair of little 0-4-4 tanks which Drummond built in 1905. Even they succumbed in the end, one finishing its career literally by shedding a driving wheel and sending it bowling along the 'six foot' until a gatepost halted progress. In replacement came almost new pannier tanks from the GWR, of all unlikely things. During the war a pair of Stroudley Class D1 0-4-2 tanks had been lent to the Highland section — one worked at Wick — but they were actually ancestors of the Dornoch 0-4-4 tanks. A Swindon pannier tank must have seemed exotic indeed, but not for long as the Dornoch line closed in 1960 after the visitors had been working it for only a short time.

The provision of 'Black Fives' to replace Highland main line engines in the 1930s caused the older ones to be scrapped, and the newer ones took over the lighter local duties. But by 1945 many of them were no longer fit even for this work, so there was a Caledonian influx. As well as doing the banking and piloting work already mentioned, CR 4-4-0s appeared on local passenger trains. There also came to the Highland some of McIntosh's '812' class standard goods 0-6-0s, some 0-6-0 shunting tanks, and the ubiquitous 0-4-4 tanks. In this matter the Highland somewhat resembled the GSWR section, but there was no great Midland invasion, although Aviemore Shed's allocation did include at least one Compound.

My introduction to the Highland was in the late 1940s. We came (shamefully) by car to the Station Hotel at Inverness. Here, surely, there would be Highland engines to see. But on that first evening none came, and I consoled myself by extensively robbing the luggage label rack where Highland relics were to be found. The company had a curious habit of referring to itself on paper as The Highland Railway, and for a while this style also appeared on the engines. Other railways of my acquaintance being content to forego the definite article, I found this Highland style novel but not unexpected in what was for me a strange land where things ought to be appreciably different. Family plans were to spend the next few days exploring the beautiful mountains and glens by car. Having seen no Highland rolling stock at all so far, and with the prospect of a rail-less holiday ahead, I was feeling disappointed as I ate my breakfast the next morning in the Hotel dining room which adjoined the station platform. In the background there were, muted, the usual railway noises. An engine whistled. I believe in films it is called a 'double take' when a character sees or hears something, takes no notice, and then realises the significance of what has just happened and reacts accordingly. It suddenly sunk in, amid the eggs and bacon, that LMS and Caledonian engines hoot. A whistle could only mean Highland. I was away from that table and my long-suffering parents with more haste than manners, bolted out into the station, and down platform 2. There at the outer end stood a 'Clan Goods', filthy and leaking steam, but at last the genuine article. It even had the front vacuum standpipe folded back down on the footplating, a trick that only Highland engines could perform. The rest of the holiday passed off peacefully, after honour had thus been satisfied.

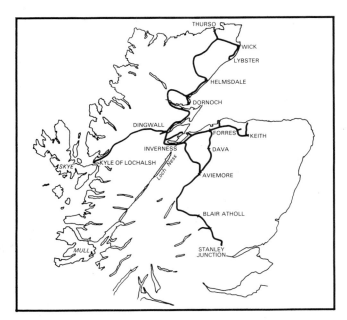

Plate 193: This elegant design of a main building without a platform awning, but having projecting wings flanking a colonnaded waiting area instead, was something of a Highland Railway standard for larger stations. A Caledonian 4-4-0 is arriving at Elgin with the stopping train from Inverness which will go on to Aberdeen, via Mulben and Keith Junction. The leading carriages are LMS, with a Gresley bogie and a van behind. The GNSR station is behind us to the right, reached by a long curved platform. It is closed now, but in 1953 was busier than this station which is the only one open in Elgin today.

Plate 194: The stone-built HR engine shed at Forres was much reduced in importance when the direct south line to Aviemore, via Slochd, was opened in 1898, but it continued to serve local needs. Standing outside its home shed in September 1954 is one of the CR '812' class 0-6-0s, No. 57620.

Photomatic

Plate 195: Although the Highland Railway line from Elgin to Keith Junction (locally called the Mulben line) was something of a poor relation when compared with the Great North of Scotland services between the two places, it alone survives as part of the Aberdeen to Inverness route. In 1953 it had only three trains daily each way, and 'Pickersgill' No. 54473 has just arrived at Keith Junction, the 'hand-over' point, with one of them. An LNER Class 'B12' 4-6-0 will take it forward to Aberdeen. GNSR section trains from Elgin, via Craigellachie, used a platform out of sight to the left.

Plate 196: The local train betwen Forres and Keith was regarded as fitting employment for one of the 'Small Ben' class, No. 14410 *Ben Dearg*, in June 1949. It is stopping at Orbliston Junction, where the line to Fochabers Town left the Keith to Elgin line. Its passenger services were withdrawn in 1931, and Orbliston itself closed in 1964, although the line through it is still open.

J.L. Stevenson

Plate 197: This 'Pickersgill' has an excess of steam and smoke as it stands at the end of the platform at Nairn, waiting to leave for Inverness. The distinctive profile of the cab roof, domed in the centre and flattened at the edges, shows up well in this picture, and we can also see a lamp on the cabside lamp iron. Before the Grouping, CR engines had no buffer beam lamp irons but carried lamps (which had side brackets and lenses fore and aft) on these cabside lamp irons. The LMS provided lamp irons on the buffer beams and suppressed the double lens lamps, so the enginemen used the cabside irons to keep their spare lamps on.

A.E. Bennett

Plate 198: A relic of the distant past at Fort George, destination of the branch from Gollanfield Junction on the Forres line. This six-wheeled hand crane had been the property of the Inverness & Aberdeen Junction Railway since 1859, or so its axlebox covers proclaimed. Its owners got their money's worth because it was still in working order in 1952, although somewhat embarrassed by weeds.

R.E. Wilson

Plate 199: Unlike the Caledonian and the GSWR, who bought their signals from Stevens & Sons of London and Glasgow, the HR made Mackenzie & Holland of Worcester their main suppliers. The fluted half-ball and long-spike finial was their distinctive trademark. In July 1952 this old wooden post signal at Gollanfield Junction was about to be replaced by a modern steel-mounted upper quadrant.

R.E. Wilson

Plate 200: Latterly the Highland Railway had a liking for vertical matchboard carriage panelling which adorns this 1916 postal tender. In 1960 it was still working over the mountains to Inverness, one of the last HR carriages still in service, but it was replaced in June of the following year.

Plate 201: The problems of train working in the Highlands are demonstrated by this assemblage at Ballinluig in 1952. There being no suitable siding, the Aberfeldy branch train has been shunted out of its rightful place beside the platform so that the 'Pickersgill', on a northbound goods, can clear the main line and be overtaken by a northbound passenger train. The Aberfeldy train seems to be well provided with brake van accommodation.

R.E. Wilson

Plate 202: Now alongside the branch platform at Ballinluig, the Aberfeldy train is waiting for mails from the south to be loaded before setting off on its nine mile run up into the hills. The engine is a CR 0-4-4 tank, No. 55212. Notice the barrows with their high wheels and side raves — genuine HR stock. Were those wheels to cope with snowbound platforms?

W.A.C. Smith

Plate 203: The station buildings at Aberfeldy are of local stone and provided with crow step gables in the authentic Scottish style. By 1957, BR stock has made its appearance on the branch, but the engine is still a Caledonian 0-4-4 tank, a class which worked the line until the diesels came in 1961. On the right there is a two-lever ground frame to operate the engine release crossover in the absence of any push and pull working. Aberfeldy closed in 1965.

A.E. Bennett

Plate 204: As we move north, the mountains are beginning to close in on the main line to Inverness. This southbound goods train is hauled by 'Pickersgill' No. 54486 from Perth Shed, where somebody thought enough of it to fix a star round the smokebox door handle and paint the hinge straps. Pressure of work during the 1960 summer season is probably why it has not been cleaned lately.

Photomatic

Plate 205: Midland Compounds were not common in the Highlands, but Perth's No. 40913 worked the morning 'stopper' to Blair Atholl in June 1953. It is in its first BR livery, plain black with block numbers, and no shed plate or evidence of ownership. A year later the engine returned to its first Scottish home, the GSWR section. Smoke in the background indicates that the southbound goods is just pulling out.

R.E. Wilson

Plate 206: The Highland Railway was once a '4-4-0 line' like the Great North of Scotland, but although the gradients soon required the HR to have something stronger to work its traffic, it retained the habit of using the current 4-4-0s for goods work, especially in summer when there could be an engine shortage north of Perth. This must account for working an engineer's train by 'Pickersgill' No. 54488, seen here shunting at Aviemore in July 1957. The rolled up storm sheet on the cab roof seems to anticipate rain.

A.E. Bennett

Plate 207: More shunting, at Boat of Garten this time, on the stretch of the 'old main line' between Aviemore and Forres which BR closed in 1965. Happily the Strathspey Railway still runs over it and they have a CR '812' Class 0-6-0 like this one, for our enjoyment. In July 1957, such engines were still common on former LMS lines in Scotland. The shunter stands behind the tender with his pole hooked into the wagon coupling, waiting to heave down on it and unhook as the engine gives the rake a brisk shove backwards.

A.E. Bennett

Plate 208: The rugged nature of the civil engineering on the direct Inverness line shows up well as this heavy passenger train battles up to Slochd Summit, piloted as usual by a 'Pickersgill', No. 54488. The 1950s was the last decade of this traditional practice. If they ever have to repair the retaining wall there will be no shortage of stone.

P. Tatlow Collection

Plate 209: The summit at Slochd is remote from any station, but a crossing loop was provided there which allowed pilot engines to be detached and return down the hill rather than go right through to Aviemore or Inverness. This CR 4-4-0 has double-headed the train on the right, and is now running light engine through the loop, no doubt to assist another train up the long stretches at 1 in 60 which lead to this isolated spot.

A.E. Bennett

Plate 210: The grand stone arch at the entrance to Inverness Shed must have been a welcome sight to many a crew after a rough trip from Perth. Standing outside in 1950 is 'Clan Goods' No. 57954, typifying the final HR engine style with outside cylinders and Walschært's valve gear. The block renumbering has not reached the tender, and the positioning on the smokebox of both number and shed plates is unusual. Note the front vacuum brake standpipe, folded down out of the way.

P. Tatlow Collection

Plate 211: A tender end view of the same engine in 1949 showing the long cab roof with a rear valance to reduce the opening against winter storms. There is a tablet exchanger on the cabside and the tender has the distinctive shield-shaped covers to its lracier-pattern axleboxes, a feature that also appeared on late HR passenger stock. For the passenger variety of this 4-6-0 *see Plate 212.*

H.C. Casserley

Plate 212: 'Handsome is as handsome does', and the 'Clan' class 4-6-0s were thought by many people to be the best-ever Highland Railway engines on both counts. Alas they did not long survive the war and No. 54767 *Clan Mackinnon* was the only one to be renumbered by BR, and was scrapped at Kilmarnock in 1950. As well as its fine looks it shows the LMS continuing the HR tradition of painting engine names, rather than having metal plates. It cannot have been weight problems — maybe it was the price of brass.

P. Tatlow Collection

Plate 213: This seven compartment matchboarded Highland Railway corridor composite, standing at Inverness in 1952, was built by Pickerings of Wishaw. Like the final Highland engines it has Iracier axleboxes.

R.E. Wilson

Plate 214: The Black Isle lies between the Moray and the Cromarty Firths, and a branch was opened to Fortrose from Muir of Ord on the north line in 1894. Passenger services were withdrawn in 1951 as road traffic revived after the war, but the goods continued to run for coal and agricultural traffic until 1960. A Caledonian 0-6-0 is seen shunting at Allangrange, the second station along the branch, in August 1959.

W.A.C. Smith

Plate 215: Fortrose was the terminus of the Black Isle branch, its passenger trains being an early casualty in the elimination of unprofitable services. In August 1948, the accommodation provided was a real mixture of old and new. No doubt 'Small Ben' No. 14399 *Ben Wyvis* felt more comfortable attached to a carriage. The loss of smokebox wingplates when a Caledonian boiler replaced its Highland original was sad, but only those of the class which received these new boilers managed to survive the war.

J.L. Stevenson

Plate 216: This Inverness-based McIntosh 0-6-0, No. 57594 would not have been able to tackle a load such as this north of Dingwall, but will be able to manage the more easily-graded line back to its home shed. Even so in July 1959 there is some heavy work ahead, unlikely the duty on the Fortrose branch shown in *Plate 214*.

P. Tatlow

Plate 217: As this 'Pickersgill' arrives at Achnasheen the bleak moorland rising above it is shrouded in mist, although it is July in 1958. This may be just an ordinary Kyle line goods, but the veteran six-wheeled brake behind the tender may indicate that it is a ballast train. Nowadays radio signalling has made semaphores and signal wires things of the past at Achnasheen and on much of the Highland line north of Inverness.

P. Tatlow

Plate 218: Strathcarron was a typical small Highland Railway signal box, built of timber and close to track level. There generally was no need for an elevated siting, there being few overbridges to obscure the view, and a low box made it easier for the signalman to get down to the tablet exchanger on its ground standard. The engine shunting the vans, No. 17951, is a 'Clan Goods', as yet unrenumbered by its new owners in June 1948.

Photomatic

Plate 219: 'Clan Goods' No. 57954 retained its original HR chimney to the end, but a Caledonian-pattern snifting valve behind the chimney has been fitted, although this class was superheated from new. In their last years they were mainly to be found on the line to the Kyle of Lochalsh, the erstwhile Dingwall & Skye Railway.
Lens of Sutton

Plate 220: The mountains on the Isle of Skye loom out of the mist as 'Clan Goods' No. 57955 shunts some passenger stock at the Kyle of Lochalsh. It may be well into the spring of 1952 but the engine still carries its small snowplough, virtually a permanent fixture during the winter months. Back in 1945 the LMS had fitted this engine not only with a Caledonian snifting valve, but also with what looks like the chimney off a departed Caledonian 4-6-0. The appearance is changed, but not ruined.
H.C. Casserley

Plate 221: The approach to the Kyle of Lochalsh from Inverness is through a rock cutting, widened to take sidings that were originally used for sheep and cattle vans, the Highland having a useful lifestock traffic from the Islands. The station pilot in July 1957 was a CR 0-4-4 tank, seen here bringing some cattle trucks under the road bridge which spans the east end of the station yard. A pair of ex-Highland carriages converted to ballast brakes — one bogie and one six-wheeled — are in the near siding.

A.E. Bennett

Plate 222: Perhaps the best-known view of the layout at the Kyle of Lochalsh is from the road bridge, with the station pilot in evidence. The station is in fact a large island platform with its buildings in the middle, and reached by a ramp from this bridge. The pier for the ferry to Kyleakin, on the Isle of Skye, is close at hand, but still far enough away for passengers to get a soaking during a storm. if they have just come off the ferry perhaps they are glad enough to have reached land not to mind the rain, because the crossing, although short, can be very rough.

A.E. Bennett

Plate 223: There has long been something of a 'local' service from Inverness as far as Tain, 44 miles out on the Far North line, and the CR 4-4-0s often worked it in the 1950s. As No. 54470 calls at Kildary, in August 1959, with the midday working south from Tain, we can study the traffic carried. The porter has flower boxes for Forres, the postman has the mails, and there are a few local passengers. On the other track first lunch is just being served in the LNER restaurant car of the 10.40a.m. Inverness to Wick and Thurso train. The car will come off at Helmsdale and then serve high teas and dinners all the way back to Inverness. Lastly, tucked away beside the modest waiting shelter, is the wooden step box for those who find Kildary's low platforms a bit of a trial.

W.A.C. Smith

Plate 224: The Mound was, I think, originally this embankment carrying the main road across the head of Loch Fleet, on its way northwards up the coast. It was widened in 1902 to carry the Dornoch Light Railway southwards towards the county town of Sutherland. The railway survived with two trains daily each way until 1960, and now the improvements to the A9 road are threatening the Far North main line as well. In April 1952, however, it was 'line clear' for the branch train behind its HR 0-4-4 tank.

H.C. Casserley

Plate 225: No. 55053 was the last Highland Railway engine in regular BR service until one of its wheels came off in 1957. It has lots of Drummond features like the integral splasher and sand box (copied from William Stroudley), dome-mounted safety-valves and the Drummond family cab. Peter Drummond's tank engines did not perpetuate the Stroudley curved upper edge to the tanks, but look at the neat way the tank-top handrail is curved round the filler cap.

H.C. Casserley

Plate 226: It is not generally known that there was an outbreak of the Caledonian disease called stovepipe chimneys on the Highland, but this view of 'Small Ben' class 4-4-0 No. 54399 confirms it. *Ben Wyvis* is piloting a 'Black Five' on the 'up' morning service from Wick and Thurso, and the two have stopped, blocking both the level crossing and the loop points at Brora in July 1951. Happily, they were not booked to cross a 'down' train there. No doubt the people of Brora were content to wait by the line until the train left.

A.J.S. Paterson

Plate 227: Apart from Wick, Helmsdale was the most northerly engine shed in Britain and it can be glimpsed between the wagons on the right and the station in the distance. In this 1949 view the main interest is 'Small Ben' class No. 14409 *Ben Alisky*, built in 1900 and never renumbered by BR. What a difference the proper chimney cap makes! Also of great interest are the HR rotating ground signal prominent on the right and the splendid Midland Railway dining car on the left, waiting for its southbound working.

H.C. Casserley

Plate 228: All Far North line trains served both Wick and Thurso, generally dividing at Georgemas Junction to do so. The Thurso portion had to reverse, because of the junction layout, and here it is being attached to a southbound train by 'Small Ben' class No. 54398 *Ben Alder* which has, on 24th April 1952, brought it to the junction. The 'down' platform from which this picture was taken continues on the right to serve the Thurso line, the Inverness platform being behind the train and reached by a Highland Railway footbridge.

H.C. Casserley